OFFICIAL
PUBLICATIONS
IN BRITAIN

OFFICIAL PUBLICATIONS IN BRITAIN

Second edition

David Butcher
Principal Lecturer, School of Information Studies, Birmingham Polytechnic

LIBRARY ASSOCIATION PUBLISHING
LONDON
A CLIVE BINGLEY BOOK

Published by
Library Association Publishing Ltd
7 Ridgmount Street
London WC1E 7AE

First published 1991

British Library Cataloguing in Publication Data

Butcher, David
    Official publications in Britain. —— 2nd ed.
    I. Title
    070.50941

    ISBN 0-85157-422-X

Typeset from author's disks in 10/12pt Times by Library Association Publishing Ltd.
Printed and made in Great Britain by Bookcraft Ltd, Midsomer Norton, Avon.

Contents

List of tables

For

Kim and Li-Li

Preface

The pattern of official publishing in Britain continues to change. This second edition aims to present a concise and up-to-date overview of the range of current official publishing. It is intended for practising librarians, students of library and information studies, and users of official publications to help them to discern the pattern of official publishing today. Her Majesty's Stationery Office is the largest single general publisher of official material, but its output represents only a small proportion of the total. The great majority of official publications are published directly by government departments, public bodies and local authorities. Despite advances in bibliographic control, some of these publications are still relatively little known and under-used. Developments in electronic publishing have begun to have a significant impact in the official publications field with online and CD-ROM databases becoming more common.

The book examines the nature and organization of official publishing in Britain at national, regional and local levels, the extent and adequacy of bibliographic control, and the ways in which these publications may be selected and acquired. Publications are discussed in the context of the functions and work of the different kinds of official bodies responsible for producing them. This approach is well established for parliamentary publications but is less frequently extended to other kinds of British official publications. The different types of publications are illustrated with recent examples. In the chapter on national and regional public bodies in particular, the work and publications of organizations selected as examples of their kind are surveyed. Chapter 5 on bibliographic control analyses the tools for tracing official publications and assesses their effectiveness. Chapter 6 looks at how official publications may be obtained and briefly outlines library provision and some issues in their organization and exploitation. Local government publishing is still the most shadowy area of official publishing, despite the volume of material produced and some improvements in publishing practice and bibliographic control. The functions of local authorities, the main types of publications they issue, and the key sources for gaining access to this material are surveyed in this self-contained final chapter.

This book does not attempt to describe what each government department or public body publishes: to do so adequately would require a much larger volume, which would rapidly become out of date. Instead it offers a structured approach to the role and output of the whole range of official bodies to help those who provide or use them to understand the nature of their publishing. The main emphasis throughout is on current publications, with more limited treatment of older material and how to trace it. Each chapter is accompanied by references to recent books, seminar papers and articles which give more extensive information on the publishing of specific organizations or on other aspects of official publishing. The scope of the book extends to the United Kingdom as a whole, with examples drawn from organizations and publishing in each of its constituent countries.

Acknowledgements are due to previous writers on official publications and to the students who opted for my official publications course over the last 15 years. My thanks to Valerie Nurcombe and Stephen Hewett for their help and comments, and to Pam Douglas for transferring most of the original text to disc. My special thanks go to my wife and collaborator who has read and discussed the contents and given her unfailing support and encouragement. All errors and omissions are my own.

David Butcher

Abbreviations

ACAS	Advisory, Conciliation and Arbitration Service
ADAS	Agricultural Development and Advisory Service
AFRC	Agricultural and Food Research Council
BBC	British Broadcasting Corporation
BC	Borough Council
BLDSC	British Library Document Supply Centre
BLRD	British Library Research and Development (Department)
BNB	*British national bibliography*
BR	British Rail
BRE	Building Research Establishment
BRTT	*British reports, translations and theses*
BSO	Business Statistics Office
BTA	British Tourist Authority
CAA	Civil Aviation Authority
CC	County Council
CNAA	Council for National Academic Awards
CoBOP	*Catalogue of British official publications not published by HMSO*
CRE	Commission for Racial Equality
CSO	Central Statistical Office
DC	District Council
DES	Department of Education and Science
DH	Department of Health
DHSS	Department of Health and Social Security
DoE	Department of the Environment
DSS	Department of Social Security
DTI	Department of Trade and Industry
DTp	Department of Transport
EC	European Community
EDM	Early Day Motion

EOC	Equal Opportunities Commission
ERDF	European Regional Development Fund
ESA-IRS	European Space Agency Information Retrieval Services
ESRC	Economic and Social Research Council
ETB	English Tourist Board
FT	*Financial times*
GLG	Government Libraries Group (Library Association)
HA	Health Authority
HC	House of Commons
HCP	House of Commons Paper
HEA	Health Education Authority
HL	House of Lords
HMSO	Her Majesty's Stationery Office
HSC	Health and Safety Commission
HSE	Health and Safety Executive
IFLA	International Federation of Library Associations
ISBN	International Standard Book Number
ISG	Information Services Group (Library Association) (formerly RSIS)
ITB	Industrial Training Board
IWAAC	Inland Waterways Amenity Advisory Council
JANET	Joint Academic Network
LA	Library Association
LB	London Borough
LRC	London Research Centre
MAFF	Ministry of Agriculture, Fisheries and Food
MBC	Metropolitan Borough Council
MDC	Metropolitan District Council
MLC	Meat and Livestock Commission
MP	Member of Parliament
MRC	Medical Research Council
MSC	Manpower Services Commission
NCC	National Consumer Council
NCET	National Council for Educational Technology
NEDC	National Economic Development Council
NEDO	National Economic Development Office
NERC	Natural Environment Research Council
NHS	National Health Service
OPCS	Office of Population Censuses and Surveys
OS	Ordnance Survey

POLIS	Parliamentary On Line Information Service
RC	Research Council
RHA	Regional Health Authority
RSIS	Reference, Special and Information Section (Library Association) (now ISG)
SCOOP	Standing Committee on Official Publications
SI	Statutory Instrument
SIGLE	System for Information on Grey Literature in Europe
SSS	Selected Subscription Service
TEED	Training, Enterprise and Education Directorate (Department of Employment Group)
UK	United Kingdom
UKOP	*The catalogue of United Kingdom official publications on CD-ROM*
V & A	Victoria and Albert Museum
WDA	Welsh Development Agency
WIB	*Weekly information bulletin* (House of Commons)
YTS	Youth Training Scheme

1 The scope and structure of official publishing in Britain

WHAT ARE OFFICIAL PUBLICATIONS?

Official publications are a very diverse group united only by their common origin in governments and their associated bodies.[1] They are major sources of information in practically every subject field and some have a special authority through being issued by the government. They require study not only for these reasons but also because of the vast quantity produced, the variety of forms in which they may appear and the different ways in which they are published. Official publications are difficult to ignore simply in quantitative terms: the United States Government Printing Office is the largest single publisher in the Western world while Her Majesty's Stationery Office (HMSO) is the most prolific general publisher in Britain. It is difficult to estimate the total British output as it depends on the definition of 'publication' as well as of what constitutes an official body. HMSO's own figure of some 9,000 titles a year, together with the 11,000 or so non-HMSO publications listed by Chadwyck-Healey suggests that about 20,000 appear each year. This excludes publishers of specialist material not covered by the Chadwyck-Healey list like the Patent Office, which alone issues nearly 25,000 individual patent specifications a year, as well as publications from local authorities.

The majority of official publications are issued in printed form as books, pamphlets, leaflets and periodicals. Every other physical form of publication is used for some official material including films and videos, sound recordings, slides, maps, microforms, CD-ROM discs and software packages. It is usually easier to trace printed materials in the bibliographies, though some lists include non-print materials. Not all British official publications are in English: the Welsh Office issues many Welsh language and bilingual publications and several other official bodies issue publications in the languages of the main ethnic minority groups in Britain.

1

Subject range and readership

Official publications contribute in varying degrees to almost every subject field. In law, education, business, building or agriculture they are of vital importance because of legislation, regulations, reports, statistics and advisory publications. In many scientific and technical fields patents and research reports from official bodies are major primary information sources. Officially published historical and archaeological works are useful to everyone from the research student to the school child. In some subjects like music, literature or philosophy the contribution of official publications is more limited.

The average person, if they think at all of official publications, would probably remember a government report or act, the *Highway code* and the leaflets on social security benefits. Yet official publications contain information which affects the life of every single person in the country through legislation, government policy decisions, reports and information publications on matters like taxation, pensions, health care, education, housing and employment, and local government publications like planning documents which directly affect the local environment.

Many official publications are aimed at the widest possible audience: school children, the amateur enthusiast, or people seeking new hobbies and leisure interests. Some are sold in large numbers: the *Highway code* is HMSO's perennial bestseller. Very occasionally documents are distributed to every household: the explanatory booklet about the Community Charge was circulated in this way in 1989. Most official publications never reach this wide potential audience though.

A substantial number of official publications are produced for a more specialized readership. For the research worker in subject fields as diverse as nuclear energy, coal mining, zoology and archaeology, official bodies sponsor investigations and publish the results. To many professionals, whether architect, solicitor, doctor, teacher or engineer, an awareness of publications from official bodies is an essential part of their knowledge of the subject and of current developments in it. For the business executive current statutes, regulations, codes of practice, statistics and export information are essential to the operations of commercial organizations.

Despite their enormous potential value official publications are often ignored or under-used. This occurs through lack of awareness of their relevance and because users of official information face barriers more severe than those for most other information sources. Official publications often seem an impenetrable mystery to the outsider or a confusing jungle to those who try to use them. Simply finding out what already exists on the topic in which they are interested is difficult enough for most users. Keeping up-to-date with relevant new official publications, especially those not published by HMSO, can be even more problematic. In most cases users need to see the document to assess its relevance as there are very few evaluative sources which help them to select what they need. Finding out where the publications can be obtained from and acquiring copies is far from easy as many official publications are not marketed and distributed professionally and are not available in bookshops. These problems can make the use of official publications frustrating and time-consuming, while delay in obtaining the information may greatly reduce its value to the user. Some understanding of the ways in which official documents are published and the organizations responsible for them is needed both by the librarian and the user if much important material is not to be overlooked.

Definition of official publications

Official publications, whatever their subject, form or readership, are produced by organizations associated with government. It is the nature of the issuing body and not the kind of information within the publication nor its physical form which determines its status as an official publication. Even publications issued by commercial publishers or other non-official bodies are normally regarded as official if they originate in official bodies. The IFLA definition of official publications[2] issued in 1983 defines official bodies as legislatures, executive agencies and courts of a state or any administrative subdivision of a state (like provincial or local authorities), together with organizations set up by and maintaining continuing links (e.g. financial, reporting) with an official body. International intergovernmental organizations are also official bodies. The extent of official publishing depends on the practice of each individual country in designating bodies as 'official'.

In the British context the main legislature is Parliament. The executive agencies include government departments which administer government policy within their own area of concern, and have specialized units and sections such as the Assessment of Performance Unit within the Department of Education and Science. The government has set up many official bodies in the form of boards, committees, councils and public corporations which are responsible for a service, industry or other function. These include executive bodies of various kinds, research organizations, and the health authorities. Advisory and consultative bodies advise the government on policy-making and comment on its actions. In Britain universities, learned societies, political parties, trade associations and independent research bodies are not regarded as being official bodies, though they may be so classified in other states. The courts of law are independent of the government in Britain and are excluded from this book, though administrative tribunals are discussed (see Chapter 4). Both types of judicial body are regarded as official in the IFLA definition.

Power is fairly heavily concentrated at the national level in Britain where most legislation, policy statements, consultative documents and information publications are issued as a result of the work of the legislature and the executive. British regional institutions are relatively weak, with nothing comparable to the individual state governments of the United States. The main regional organizations like the regional health authorities, arts boards and tourist boards are all linked to government departments or other official bodies. The main units of government below the national level are the local authorities, each of which administers a particular area under powers delegated to them by Parliament. Many official organizations of all kinds are publishers of information: for some, indeed, this is the main justification for their existence. The British pattern of official publishing can be seen alongside that of its European neighbours in the two-volume survey of *Official publications of Western Europe*.[3]

The availability of official information is also affected by different views of what constitutes a 'publication'. Under legal deposit regulations a work is a publication if it is issued to the public, however limited the number of copies distributed. When reprographic facilities were not so widely available within organizations a printed document was normally a publication for wide circulation, while material in typewriter script would usually be for internal use within the organization. Today the situation is much less clear-cut. Many official bodies produce what are essentially internal documents, some copies of which may be circulated to interested organizations and individuals, but which are not always regarded as publications by their producers. Other documents like circulars and letters are mainly for restricted circulation to local authorities and other official bodies. There is a grey area of semi-published material such as research reports and technical studies which may be circulated only to a very limited audience. Even a document which is officially published may not be widely available: only 250 copies of Sir Douglas Black's report on *Inequalities in health* (DHSS, 1981) were

4

printed and there was no distribution to the press, radio or television (it was subsequently published by Penguin, however). The definition of 'publication' is important because it affects which official documents can be traced in bibliographies, as many exclude semi-published and unpublished material.

Why do official bodies publish?

Official organizations issue publications for a variety of reasons. The government has a constitutional duty to publish laws and regulations to inform citizens of their duties, rights and responsibilities. Informed citizens who are aware of the important issues and who can debate the merits of government policies are fundamental to participatory democracy, in which governments are accountable for their actions to their citizens. They need access to the discussions of the legislature and information on policy decisions. By informing Parliament the government informs the electorate as a whole. Many governments consult the public or interested groups before taking final policy decisions and issue discussion documents and background studies on each topic. The pressure of public opinion has resulted in the increased availability of such information. When final decisions on policy have been taken these must be announced and their implications explained. Most people hear about government policy through newspapers, periodicals, radio and television, but these reports are very brief summaries and may be biased or inaccurate. The full document must be published and needs to be easily available to those wishing to consult it.

Governments not only need to publish legislation and policy decisions but also to explain in clear language what they mean and how people will be affected. Most official bodies are required to produce regular reports and statistics on their work so that they are subject to public scrutiny. A major incentive to publishing for many official bodies is to make known the facilities and services they offer and to explain their work. This is particularly important for government departments, the remaining nationalized industries and official bodies promoting interest in their area of concern. Another factor is the need to disseminate some of the vast amount of information collected and held by the government so that it can be used by a wider public, though this is seen as subsidiary to the needs of government itself. Much of this information is unique, like the population census data or industrial production statistics. Official bodies fund research work, enquiries and studies which must be published if their results are to be used. Finally, official bodies have built up expert knowledge in their subject which can be used to offer information and advice to the public partly through leaflets, booklets and more substantial publications.

Government information policy

These reasons for publishing should not be taken to imply that governments necessarily have any overall information policy. A fundamental problem affecting the dissemination of official information in Britain is the ambivalence of the government's attitude. The policies which have emerged in the 1980s from the report of the Information Technology Advisory Panel, *Making a business of information*, and the government response to it view information almost wholly in economic terms.[4, 5] Government-held information is a commodity to be bought by businesses or a product they can trade. Its release was seen as valuable support for the UK information industry, which could be stimulated by public/private sector interaction. Government departments should not compete with private sector services nor introduce services which might be offered by the private sector. Where government departments do provide information they should take a commercial approach.[6, 7] The government did recognize that a substantial amount of central and local government information will continue to be free or subsidized for non-commercial users. It has not, however, considered the wider issues involved in disseminating the information it holds, only some economic factors.

While tradeable information is developing partly through electronic sources, the policies also affect printed publications. These are to be sold at a profit wherever possible through HMSO's sales organization or by the private sector. There seems to have been little consideration of the effects of pricing on the availability of official publications to individuals and libraries, obvious though these are. On the other hand, official bodies set up public relations sections and may make considerable and expensive efforts to ensure that the information they produce is widely distributed. These individual efforts often fail because the organizations concerned lack the means of effective distribution that HMSO possesses. As a result priced official information is published and made available fairly widely on a systematic basis while dissemination by other official bodies is more haphazard.

Availability of official information

Official information is a much broader term than 'official publication'

6

and includes much that is not published in the conventional way. Several Western governments have made official information more widely available. In Britain freedom of information legislation has been implemented for access to local government information and some types of health information but not in respect of central government information. The government views information as its own property. To a considerable extent it determines what people should know in this country and when they are told it. The Central Policy Review Staff's study on pensions in 1983 was suppressed because of the possibility of a general election, yet its proposals are the basis of current pensions law. The extent of concealment from the public of the facts about both the leaks of radioactive material from the Windscale (now Sellafield) nuclear reactor before the 1957 fire and the seriousness of the fire itself has only become apparent more than 30 years later. There is a strong tendency in central government to keep as much as possible confidential. Access is still restricted in fields like food, environmental, safety or health information. The official secrets legislation has been amended to take disclosure of much official information outside the scope of the criminal law but is in some respects more restrictive.

Even when information is published, the way in which it is presented may be manipulated to show the government and its policies in the best light. This is clearest with press releases, some of which are overt propaganda. Political documents like government policy statements are carefully written to stress the benefits of the policies. A factual source like *Britain: an official handbook* is compiled by government departments and noticeably reflects the government's policies and viewpoint in its descriptions of the British way of life. Experienced users of official publications learn to read between the lines!

Another factor affecting the availability of official information in Britain is the restriction of some types of information sources to particular groups. Several kinds of information which were publicly available at the beginning of the 1980s are now restricted. Much agricultural advisory material from the Agricultural Development and Advisory Service (ADAS) is now only issued to ADAS clients and colleges of agriculture, while most export information from the Department of Trade and Industry is limited to exporters. A broader and more serious question which has emerged recently is how far official information in electronic form is effectively unavailable to potential users because of high access costs or lack of the skills required to exploit this information.

Table 1   The structure of British official publishing

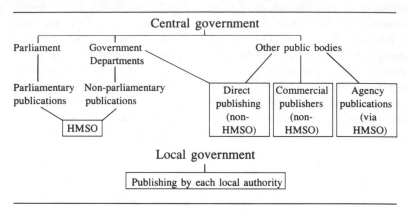

HER MAJESTY'S STATIONERY OFFICE

The pattern of publishing and methods of distribution of official publications have a significant effect on the ease with which they can be obtained and used. HMSO is the only large-scale centralized official publisher in Britain. It publishes about 9,000 new titles a year, though this figure is inflated as it counts each issue of a periodical as a separate publication.

HMSO as publisher

HMSO has an almost complete monopoly of publishing on behalf of Parliament which accounts for nearly half its output. It produces the debates, reports, bills and acts arising from the work of both Houses and the publications required by Parliament for the examination of government activities and policies. Statutory material (mainly statutory instruments and *Statutes in force*) form a significant part of the non-parliamentary publications and represent about a quarter of HMSO's total output. The balance consists of non-parliamentary publications from government departments and other public bodies, including a wide range of reports, statistics and information papers. HMSO also sells, but does not publish, agency publications on behalf of major international organizations and some British official bodies.

HMSO was founded in 1786 as a government department to supply stationery for official use.[8] It arranged for official material to be printed and later became a publisher from the mid-19th century when 'Stationery Office publications' were introduced. Publishing is a relatively small part

8

of its activities accounting for about one-seventh of its income. Its main business is still the supply of stationery, equipment and printing requirements for government departments and other public bodies.

HMSO is the largest general publisher in the UK in number of titles though not in sales volume. It has much less control over what it publishes than most commercial publishers. Material required by Parliament and statutory publications must be published. Government ministers and civil servants decide how material is to be published.[9] For routine publications, like research reports, most statistics and advisory publications, departmental officials will decide whether they should be offered to HMSO as non-parliamentary publications or be published directly by the department. Publication of material which is more politically sensitive and concerns government policies will be determined by ministers. They will take a political decision on the method of publication. This accounts for a rare instance of a Command Paper not published by HMSO when the report on the Barlow Clowes investigation (Cm.671) was published by the Department of Trade and Industry in 1988.

HMSO has publishing agreements with major government departments for most non-parliamentary publications. They offer HMSO all material where the print run of sale copies exceeds 500.[10] HMSO rarely turns down material, as long as specialist items are balanced with more popular titles. Recently HMSO has commissioned some titles on its own initiative and has sought out titles from government departments and other public bodies. In 1989, for instance, it took over from the Department of Transport a series of *Transport statistics reports* which it considered marketable. It also now publishes a number of titles for such organizations as the National Consumer Council, the Museums and Galleries Commission and the Equal Opportunities Commission.

HMSO works to much shorter production schedules than commercial publishers for many of its titles. Parliamentary publications are issued on a specific day and time which may allow only days or even hours for their printing and distribution. Non-parliamentary publications are usually produced over a much longer period and may be delayed by the pressure of parliamentary publishing. Unlike most commercial publishers, HMSO has a very large number of older publications still in print: about 50,000 titles are currently available, although about a fifth are international agency publications. No HMSO publication is completely unobtainable as photocopies of out of print titles can be supplied by the British Library Document Supply Centre.

Pricing policy

Three different pricing methods are used for HMSO publications. Parliamentary publications are priced on a scale according to the number of pages. Most non-parliamentary publications are priced on a mark up of production cost plus royalty, but some titles are priced on the basis of what the market will bear. HMSO's publishing has changed in the last decade, with greater emphasis on financial return since it became a trading fund in 1980. Until then HMSO was funded by a vote of money from Parliament and did not charge government departments for printing and publishing services. HMSO now takes the financial risk on publishing and is required to make a return on its capital investment. It charges departments for goods and services supplied, though they are free to buy elsewhere. In late 1988 HMSO became an executive agency which has reinforced its commercial policy, not least because the Treasury set it higher financial targets. Government departments as well as HMSO want to increase the revenue they generate from publications. The Central Statistical Office receives royalties on its titles under a special arrangement with HMSO.

Prices of many publications increased substantially following introduction of the trading fund but they have since gone up by well below the general rate of book price inflation. Even so, prices of basic sources can be daunting: to buy a set of the acts passed in just one year cost £310 in 1990 (for the 1988 volumes). Higher prices have resulted in shorter print runs for many titles and the discontinuation of some. *Hansard* has been priced at below cost to preserve sales and the loss is financed by a government grant, but no other title is subsidized. Despite this the Commons *Hansard* cost £1,020 for the daily parts and the Lords *Hansard* £585 in 1991. Pricing policy is a matter of concern as high prices effectively reduce the availability of official publications. The real purchasing power of bookfunds in many libraries has fallen substantially in the 1980s, reducing the range of material they can provide. Reduced demand leads to higher prices or to the information becoming inaccessible because it is no longer published.

HMSO has so far been able to carry the cost of unprofitable parliamentary publications which it is obliged to publish. It also has to bear the storage costs for titles it is legally bound to keep in print, such as current acts and statutory instruments. HMSO seeks to reduce costs where possible, usually by reproducing specialist material direct from typescript or disc supplied by the author. In this way it can produce a substantial report like the Communication Steering Group's *The infra-*

structure for tomorrow (1988) for £2.95. More significantly, HMSO began testing an optical disc system in 1989 which could lead to printing on demand for items with low sales potential like most statutory instruments. This would produce substantial savings in both printing and warehousing costs. It can also speed delivery for urgent orders by using facsimile transmission, though at present its SCANFAX service is restricted to European Community material. Increased application of information technology is an important element in helping HMSO to reduce costs and meet higher government financial targets.

HMSO as printer and bookseller

HMSO is more than just a publisher: it designs and markets, distributes and often prints its own publications. HMSO's Graphic Design section has a distinguished record for the high standard of design of many official publications. Its titles are regularly selected as examples of the best of British book design in the annual British Book Design and Production exhibitions. The Publicity Section actively promotes titles through catalogues, subject lists and advertisements. The Bibliographic Section is responsible for the HMSO database and produces an extensive range of lists and catalogues for booksellers, libraries and other users. HMSO has its own presses for parliamentary printing, passports and security work, though most other printing is placed with commercial printers. It also arranges for the design and printing of many publications issued directly by government departments and other public bodies. This is a potential source of confusion as these titles may be mistaken for HMSO's own publications. However, they can be identified because they do not have the HMSO imprint on the title page nor the ISBN prefix 010 or 011.

HMSO is involved in wholesale and retail bookselling for its own publications and those for which it acts as agent. It runs six bookshops in London and major cities where the public can see many current titles and order others. Forty commercial booksellers in other parts of the country are official agents for HMSO publications. They keep a number of titles in stock and use special order facilities to supply others. Many booksellers stock a more limited range of popular HMSO publications and a substantial proportion of its sales are through the book trade. Distribution has improved dramatically since the opening of HMSO's Publications Centre in 1983 with delivery time greatly reduced. HMSO is unusual as a government publisher in having a network of agents in over 30 countries, though their stocks are very limited. HMSO's order plans are discussed in Chapter 6 and its lists and catalogues in Chapter 5.

NON-HMSO OFFICIAL PUBLISHING

HMSO has never been the sole organization issuing official publications in Britain. It was not until the early 20th century that it took over full responsibility for parliamentary publications, which were previously issued by commercial publishers. Even from 1920 to 1945, when HMSO was closest to being a monopoly publisher, some government department material was issued by other publishers. In addition, the Ordnance Survey, the Patent Office and a number of bodies such as the United Kingdom Atomic Energy Authority have a long history of publishing their own maps, patents, reports, books and pamphlets. This caused few problems for libraries and users as HMSO was responsible for legislation, official reports and other publications concerned with policy-making and government action. The non-HMSO organizations comprised a fairly small number of bodies each publishing in a specialized field and well-known to most people likely to want their publications. Within the last 40 years, however, HMSO has again lost its near monopoly position and many important policy-making documents, reports and circulars as well as a wide range of other publications are issued directly by government departments and other official bodies. The scale of non-HMSO official publishing has grown enormously, especially since the 1960s. Stephen Richard compared the number of publications recorded in the HMSO catalogues with the total official publications received by the British Library and the Bodleian Library.[11] His figures showed that whereas in 1950 40% of the 10,000 official items received by the British Library were HMSO publications, by 1966 only 14% of the 33,000 items received were from HMSO.

Factors encouraging non-HMSO publishing

This change in the pattern of official publishing has been produced by a combination of factors. The widespread availability of reprographic facilities within official organizations, particularly photocopiers and laser printers, has greatly simplified the physical production of publications. The use of word processors and desktop publishing packages has aided the preparation of accurate and easily updated master copies for reproduction. Not the least of the advantages of in-house printing is speed of issue, especially when compared with the time taken by HMSO to produce many non-parliamentary publications.

The need for government departments and other official bodies to produce kinds of publications not suited to HMSO's publishing and bookselling operations is another major factor. Many titles have very short print runs which are well below the HMSO minimum of 500 copies: most Home Office statistical bulletins, for instance, have sales of less than 50 copies. Free promotional literature is of great importance to many official bodies in making known their work and services; free advisory leaflets and brochures are prepared for widespread distribution; specialized reports of research work or consultants' studies need to be disseminated to a limited audience. None of these are likely to be handled by HMSO which deals with priced publications likely to attract fairly large sales. There has been a considerable expansion of publishing directly by government departments, which are not compelled to publish through HMSO. The amount published in this way now greatly outnumbers HMSO publications for government departments. HMSO remains responsible for the design and printing of many of these publications, but not for their publication and distribution.

Perhaps the most significant factor in the erosion of HMSO's responsibility for British official publications has been the emergence of new executive, advisory and other bodies, many of which have their own substantial publishing programmes. These official bodies differ considerably in their size, responsibilities and publishing output. Some are important concerns operating a nationalized industry or other specialized service like British Rail or the Forestry Commission. Some are promotional bodies such as the Arts Council or the tourist boards which stimulate activity and give information and advice partly through their publications. Others carry out research in a specialized field, the results of which must be communicated. Advisory bodies form the largest group but the majority issue only a few publications. Most of these organizations have no obligation to publish through HMSO and may have no opportunity to use its services. This has resulted in a large number of separate sources for official publications.

Publishing and distribution methods

The methods of publication and distribution used by government departments and other official bodies are varied. There is no single centralized publishing organization, nor can most of their publications be seen in bookshops: each body is responsible for its own publishing arrangements. HMSO does issue the annual report or accounts and sometimes other publications of certain bodies, especially the reports of some advisory bodies. A few organizations, including the Atomic Energy Research Establishment and English Heritage, use HMSO's agency arrangement to sell their publications through HMSO bookshops.

Some large-scale organizations have their own publishing subsidiary which operates like a commercial publisher and promotes publications through the book trade: BBC Books and the British Museum Press are examples. Quite a number of official bodies now cooperate with one or more commercial publishers to ensure wider distribution for some or all of their publications. The Countryside Commission and some of the national museums and galleries co-publish with publishers like Michael Joseph, Webb and Bower, Aurum Press and Phaidon. Several of the research councils and other research bodies use appropriate specialist periodicals to disseminate their research findings.

Even when an organization takes sole responsibility for its own publications the method of distribution can vary. Some have one central point for all enquiries about publications: often this is the library or the public relations department. This arrangement is the most helpful for outside enquirers, but in large organizations like government departments it is almost impossible to achieve. Publications are often distributed from individual sections or divisions rather than centrally and these must be contacted directly if material is to be obtained. The Department of Trade and Industry, for instance, has several divisions including the Overseas Trade Division and the Radio Communications Division, each issuing publications from a different address. Many large organizations, including government departments and some executive bodies, have a regional structure. A significant amount of material may be published in the regions and be available only from the region concerned: these publications can be particularly difficult to trace and obtain. Very few non-HMSO publications are available in bookshops, and many official publishers do not offer a trade discount on their priced publications. Libraries may be the only public source where they are available, yet the variety of distribution methods makes it hard even for libraries to acquire this material.

Value of non-HMSO publications

Non-HMSO official publishing at the national level is decentralized and many publications are difficult to acquire, yet they cannot simply be dismissed as ephemeral or unimportant. Several types of publication, including annual reports, consultative papers, enquiry and advisory reports and statistics may appear as parliamentary, non-parliamentary or non-HMSO publications. The distinction between them lies in the method of publication and distribution rather than in the nature of the documents themselves. There are, of course, different emphases in

14

HMSO and non-HMSO publishing such as the absence of free publications and the smaller amount of highly specialized material from HMSO. Some HMSO and rather more non-HMSO publications scarcely have an aura of 'officialness' about them. Few people would consider the *Radio times* and *Eastenders: the inside story* to be official publications, yet they are published by a subsidiary of a public corporation, the BBC. This illustrates the fact that the range of official publishing is extremely wide and the organizations involved are very diverse.

Electronic information sources

A growing amount of government information has become available in electronic form during the 1980s. The trend started modestly with a range of current information about Parliament, government departments and their services and new HMSO titles on Prestel. This now amounts to over 10,000 pages of information, including selected statistics, sources of careers information, help for small businesses, and details of the Ombudsmen. A *Guide to government services* is available on Prestel or in print to ease access to this material.

Several government departments and other official bodies have made available databases through online hosts like DataStar, ESA-IRS and FT Profile. The majority of these are bibliographic: the DHSS-DATA database of the holdings of the Department of Health and Social Security library on DataStar or HSELINE from the Health and Safety Executive on DataStar and ESA-IRS are examples. Only a limited amount of British statistical data is available online and the major source, the Central Statistical Office Databank of macro-economic and financial data is accessible through specialized hosts and via the Joint Academic Network (JANET). A few reference and factual databases are online like UKTM, the British trademarks database from the Patent Office, and Spearhead, the 1992 European Single Market database from the Department of Trade and Industry which summarizes European Community measures affecting businesses.[12]

By the late 1980s the number of databases available as CD-ROM discs began to grow rapidly and some databases from official bodies became available in this form. Notable examples include UKOP, the current bibliography of HMSO and non-HMSO official publications, and OSH-ROM, the international health and safety disc. This combines entries from the UK Health and Safety Executive, the US National Institute for Occupational Health and Safety, and the International Labour Organization's International Occupational Safety and Health Information

Centre. Relatively few reference or statistical databases on CD-ROM have yet been produced in Britain: the Post Office's *Post code address file* and Chadwyck-Healey's *1981 census: small area statistics for England, Wales and Scotland* are available. Hansard on CD-ROM is a joint venture between HMSO and Chadwyck-Healey offering the full text of Commons debates since the 1988/89 session, updated three times a year. HMSO is cooperating with Context Ltd for a CD-ROM database of statutory instruments from 1987. Other countries have also produced parliamentary debates, legislation, census data and economic statistics on CD-ROM. The National Portrait Gallery in Washington DC even has over 3,000 portraits from its permanent collection on CD-ROM. Some other British official bodies are taking advantage of developments in optical discs and document imaging. The Patent Office is developing TRIMS, a document imaging system for trademarks which allows searching by a wide range of parameters including subject area, shape and lettering as well as registered trademark number. Official information in electronic form is likely to be of increasing significance and online databases will continue to be made available through commercial hosts because of their computing facilities and established user base.

NORTHERN IRELAND

Northern Ireland had a separate but parallel pattern of official publishing from 1921, when its own Parliament was established, until 1972 when direct rule from Westminster was introduced. Its Parliament (Stormont) was subordinate to the UK Parliament and the province continued to send MPs to Westminster. Debates, journals, parliamentary papers and legislation were published separately by HMSO in Belfast. Northern Ireland government departments published non-parliamentary publications through HMSO in Belfast, and issued some material directly themselves.

Since 1972 Northern Ireland has had no separate legislature, although an elected Assembly had a consultative role between 1982 and 1986. As a consequence, legislation covering Northern Ireland is now contained in acts passed by the UK Parliament (some of them applying specifically to the province, like the Fair Employment (Northern Ireland) Act 1989) and in Orders in Council made under the Northern Ireland Act 1974. These are collected as the *Northern Ireland statutes* published by HMSO since 1973. Secondary legislation made by government departments in Northern Ireland is published as statutory rules and has been included in the monthly and annual *List of statutory instruments* since 1983. The six Northern Ireland government departments and other official bodies in the province continue to publish partly through HMSO in Belfast. Until 1986 these publications appeared in separate monthly and annual lists; they are now included in HMSO's monthly and annual catalogues. Over 100 titles a year appear in this way; they are obtainable only from the HMSO bookshop in Belfast. Non-HMSO publications are also produced and many of these are listed in the *Catalogue of British official publications*. Northern Ireland publications are discussed in the study of Irish official publishing by Maltby and McKenna.[13] Guides to publications before 1972 are referred to in Chapter 5.

References and further reading

1 The structure and importance of official publishing are discussed in: Cherns, J., *Official publishing: an overview*, Pergamon Press, 1979.
2 Johansson, E. 'The definition of official publications', *IFLA journal*, 8 (3), 1982, 282 – 90 and 8 (4), 1982, 393 – 5. 'Definition of official publications for international use', *IFLA Official Publications Section newsletter*, 12, Feb. 1984, 7 – 8. (The definition and notes are reprinted in *Whitehall and Westminster: proceedings of the seminar on official publications, London, 21 March 1984*, edited by Valerie J. Nurcombe, Library Association, Reference, Special and Information Section, 1984, 2 – 3).
3 *Official publications of Western Europe* edited by Eve Johansson, Mansell, 1984, 1988. 2 vols. (British official publishing is summarized in volume 2, 209 – 45).
4 Information Technology Advisory Panel, *Making a business of information: a survey of new opportunities*, HMSO, 1983.
5 Department of Trade and Industry, *Government response to the ITAP report on 'Making a business of information'*, HMSO, 1984.
6 Department of Trade and Industry, *Government-held tradeable information: guidelines for government departments in dealing with the private sector*, DTI, 1986.
7 The issues of tradeable information and the availability of official information are discussed in: Allan, A., *The myth of government information*, Library Association Publishing, 1990. (Viewpoints in LIS 6).
8 A useful overview of the history of HMSO and the changes of the 1980s is provided by: Barty-King, H., *Her Majesty's Stationery Office: the story of the first 200 years 1786-1986*, HMSO, 1986;

and Richardson, J., 'Her Majesty's Stationery Office', *British book news*, December 1989, 30−3.

9 Howard, B., 'Introduction and overview of British official publishing' in *Who publishes official information on health, safety and social services?* edited by Valerie J. Nurcombe, Library Association, Information Services Group, SCOOP, 1989, 5−9. Also, Penn, C., 'The role of HMSO in official publishing', *ibid.*, 10−17.

10 Brookes, P., 'A review of British official publishing − HMSO', in *Who publishes official information for business and industry?* edited by Valerie J. Nurcombe, Library Association, Information Services Group, SCOOP, 1989, 45−50.

11 Richard, S., *Directory of British official publications*, 2nd ed., Mansell, 1984, ix−x.

12 Deft, P., 'Spearhead' in *British official publications online* edited by Valerie J. Nurcombe, Library Association, Information Services Group, ISG, SCOOP, 1990, 39−44.

13 Maltby, A. and McKenna, B., *Irish official publications*, Pergamon Press, 1980.

2 *Parliamentary publications*

PARLIAMENT

The British Parliament has evolved over many centuries, transforming the country from an absolute, feudal monarchy to a parliamentary democracy in the process. The constitution in this country is a mixture of legislation, common law, custom and precedent which can be adapted to changing conditions. Unlike the American or French constitutions it is not a written document defining precisely the rights of citizens and the system of government. Parliament, consisting of the Sovereign (whose role is largely formal), the House of Lords and the House of Commons, is the supreme legislative body. The party which can control a majority of votes in the House of Commons forms the government and puts into effect its policies and legislation during its term of office.

To understand the range of publications arising from the work of Parliament a grasp of its role and functions is essential. A succinct account of these is provided in *Britain: an official handbook* (HMSO, annual).[1] Parliament's main roles are to consider and pass legislation, to examine government policies and the way in which they are administered by government departments and other public bodies, to consent to taxation to provide the money for the government's programme, and to debate major political issues.

The House of Commons

The House of Commons consists of 650 members representing constituencies throughout the United Kingdom who are elected for a period of up to five years. The life of a Parliament is divided into sessions normally lasting from November to the following October, unless Parliament is dissolved and an election called. Each session begins with the Queen's speech to Parliament outlining the government's programme and priorities for the session. This is followed by six days of debate on the speech. The House of Commons meets from Monday to Friday each week for about 170 days a session, with adjournments for holidays. Each day's sitting commences at 2.30 pm with prayers and private business (usually bills) and is normally adjourned at 10.30 pm (11 am-4.30 pm on Fridays). In the morning MPs may be taking part in committee meetings, preparing speeches or attending to constituency and other business. The first main item of business in the Commons is Question Time (except Fridays) when government ministers, and on two days a week the Prime Minister, face oral questions from MPs. Occasionally there may be a ministerial statement on a matter of government policy or reports on meetings of the European Community Council of Ministers following Question Time. The House will then debate current bills, a function which takes up over a third of its time. The subject for debate originates as a motion (proposal) which is considered and voted on. Debates take place not only on legislation but on any motion accepted by the House. These can include examination of government policy, financial business, and any other matter of concern, domestic or foreign. By 10 pm the formal business of the day has normally been concluded and half an hour remains for an adjournment debate on a topic raised by an individual MP, with a reply by a minister. In practice the House often sits until midnight or later because of pressure of business. On some Fridays time is allocated for business put forward by individual MPs and Private Members' Bills are discussed. On 20 days each session the Opposition chooses the subjects for debate. The Speaker, elected by MPs, controls debates but takes no part in them.

The House of Lords

This is the second Chamber, its membership consisting of hereditary peers, the archbishops and senior bishops of the Church of England, the Lords of Appeal (or 'law lords') and nearly 400 life peers. The potential membership is well over a thousand but about 320 attend regularly. The Lords meet on Monday to Thursday each week, with additional sittings in busier periods, for about 150 days a session. They deal with a smaller number of questions (as most are for written answer) but spend longer on examining bills, approving secondary legislation, and debating topics brought before them. The Lord Chancellor, who is a government minister, presides over the House but can take part in debates and vote.

The government

Most of the business considered by both Houses is determined by the government, the group of ministers drawn from the party with a majority in the Commons. The Prime Minister is the most powerful minister and chooses the other ministers, assigning them responsibility for a government department or other duties. Ministers are accountable to Parliament for the activities of their department. The majority of ministers are appointed from the Commons, but some are always drawn from the Lords. The most senior ministers are selected as members of the Cabinet, an inner council which takes collective responsibility for the government's policies and coordinates the work of government departments. Its deliberations are confidential, despite occasional leaks, and no record is available until the Cabinet papers are released after 30 years. The policy decided in Cabinet is introduced into Parliament for discussion and approval, particularly of the finance necessary to put it into effect.

TYPES OF PUBLICATIONS

HMSO has a virtual monopoly of publishing on behalf of Parliament and parliamentary publications account for about half of its output. These publications arise partly from the work of Parliament itself: the records of meetings of both Houses and of their various committees which examine the activities of government departments, current legislation and a range of other topics, and the records of what is said in Parliament. Legislation is introduced by the government or by individual MPs for consideration by Parliament. Other publications originate outside Parliament and are presented to it by being issued as parliamentary publications if it is essential that MPs should be acquainted with their contents. This group includes government policy proposals, treaties with other countries, reports of committees, annual reports and statistics, and other papers produced by direction of either House.

Parliamentary publications are issued in conventional categories, some of which include both those resulting from the work of Parliament and those introduced into it from outside. The appearance of parliamentary publications changed little for many years until the adoption of A4 format as the new standard size in the 1980s. At the same time charts, diagrams and colour illustrations were introduced to improve the presentation of some papers. The annual *Statement on the defence estimates* now uses colour graphics to present the case for defence spending, for instance. Electronic publishing of parliamentary material is technically possible since HMSO makes extensive use of computer typesetting, and *Hansard* in full text form became available on CD-ROM in 1991.

Table 2 Parliamentary publications

Parliamentary business
  Weekly information bulletin
  Sessional information digest
  Votes and proceedings (HC)
  Minutes of proceedings (HL)
  Journals (HC and HL)

Records of debate
  Parliamentary debates (*Hansard*) – HC and HL
  Standing Committee debates (HC)

Parliamentary papers

House of Commons bills	House of Commons
House of Commons papers	sessional papers
Command Papers	
House of Lords bills	House of Lords
House of Lords papers	sessional papers

Acts of Parliament
  Public General Acts
  Local and Personal acts

Parliamentary business

Weekly information bulletin

Since 1978 the House of Commons *Weekly information bulletin* (WIB) has provided an invaluable record of business before the House. It summarizes the previous week's business and the programme for the coming week. It is the key printed source for tracing the state of progress on each bill introduced in the session and records the membership and meetings of parliamentary committees. WIB is the most convenient source for details of recent policy statements, consultative papers and European Communities COM documents received. It has established itself as an essential tool for anyone who needs to find out what is going on in Parliament.

Sessional information digest

The *Sessional information digest*, prepared annually by the Public Information Office of the House of Commons, acts as an index and companion to WIB but does not wholly supersede it. It cumulates some of the information in WIB, like the full list of bills for the session, and indexes all consultative documents under subject headings. It provides useful statistics relating to parliamentary business, such as the time spent on government bills or adjournment debates.

The Public Information Office also produces a helpful series of nearly 60 free factsheets about parliamentary practices and procedures. Examples include *Standing Committees* (No. 43, 1987) and *Some traditions and customs of the House of Commons* (No. 52, 1988). A much smaller series relating to the House of Lords is issued by the Information Office of the House of Lords. Neither series is available from HMSO.

Votes and proceedings/Minutes of proceedings

The House of Commons *Votes and proceedings* and the House of Lords *Minutes of proceedings* are published daily, mainly for MPs. They are little used outside Parliament. Both outline the business transacted at the previous day's sitting and give the programme for the next sitting. They are equivalent to the minutes and agenda papers of any formal committee. Division lists are also included, showing how MPs voted on each motion before Parliament. Accompanying the *Votes and proceedings* are details of Commons amendments to bills, which are not available separately (unlike Lords' amendments). Finally, notices of motions will be found here, especially the Early Day Motions (EDMs) by which MPs can draw attention to a cause or pursue a campaign. The use of EDMs has grown enormously in the 1980s, though the motions are not debated: almost 1,500 were tabled during the 1989–90 session.

Journals

The *Journals*, one for each House, are compiled from the daily *Votes* and *Minutes* and form the permanent record of the business dealt with in each session of Parliament, though they do not report what is said. The *Journals* date back to 1547 for the Commons and 1510 for the Lords. Each new sessional volume is published about two years after the end of the session. Cumulative indexes covering the *Journals* from their beginnings (decennially since 1880–90) make retrospective searching easier.

Records of debates

Hansard

Virtually every word spoken in both Houses of Parliament is recorded in the *Parliamentary debates ... official report* (popularly known as *Hansard*) published daily in separate parts for each House. It is compiled by teams of shorthand reporters, computer typeset, and printed overnight for distribution next day. If, as commonly happens, Parliament sits after 10.30 pm the later debates are carried over to the next issue of *Hansard*. The Commons *Hansard* begins with the day's oral questions to ministers. These tend to be opportunities for political point scoring, especially at Prime Minister's Question Time. Each questioner is allowed a supplementary question without giving notice of the topic to the minister. MPs put down about 25,000 questions for oral answer each session, but fewer than 10% of these are answered during Question Time. The major portion of each day's *Hansard* records the speeches in debates on legislation or topical matters. The final section reports the short adjournment debate. The Lords *Hansard* contains fewer oral questions, which are limited to a small number each day, and consists mainly of the discussion of legislation, which takes up about half of its time, and other debates.

The answers to written questions, together with oral questions for which there was insufficient time, appear in each issue of the Commons *Hansard* but are separately paginated. Up to 50,000 written replies per session are given in this way. These questions can be a valuable way of gaining information about the government's intentions and actions, as well as facts and figures not easily found elsewhere. The decision to keep the Settle-Carlisle railway line open was announced to Parliament by the minister in answer to a written question, for instance. Questions can also be used to air constituency problems or to press the government to follow a particular course of action.

Hansard is published daily, in weekly collections which are found in many libraries, and in permanent bound volumes each covering two or three weeks of debates. The Commons *Hansard* is also available as a CD-ROM disc covering all debates since the 1988/89 session and updated three times a year. It is much the most convenient way of tracing an answer to a written question, a contribution to a debate or a ministerial statement. For users relying on the printed version searching is more time-consuming, although both Lords and Commons *Hansards* have separate indexes: weekly for the Lords and fortnightly for the Commons.

The Commons indexes use subject terms drawn from the POLIS thesaurus.[2] Name indexing for questions and speakers in debates is thorough. References to written questions are now clearly distinguished by a 'w' following the column reference. Indexes to each bound volume of *Hansard* and a sessional index are also published. Unlike the Commons, each Lords *Hansard* index within the session is cumulative, replacing the previous one. Verbatim records of parliamentary debates are available since 1909. Before then *Hansard* and other records of debates give only abbreviated versions of speeches.

The printed *Hansard* has a relatively small circulation, but summaries of the day's proceedings in newspapers like *The Times* have a bigger readership. Sound and video recordings and live broadcasts bring parliamentary proceedings to life and reach a much wider audience. The proceedings of the House of Lords have been televised since 1985, but the Commons has only allowed in the television cameras since late 1989. Extracts used in news bulletins are for most people the only knowledge they have of what is going on in Parliament.

Standing Committee debates

The debates of the various Standing Committees which consider bills during their committee stage (see next section) and other legislation are also recorded verbatim and published as a separate series of *Parliamentary debates. House of Commons official report.* From the 1990—91 session three European Standing Committees have replaced the previous standing committees on European Community documents to allow more effective examination of the EC proposals referred to them by the House. Six standing committees are designated to scrutinize statutory instruments. Standing committees do not have a permanent membership: they are set up anew for each item they examine. Daily parts giving the discussion at each sitting on a particular piece of legislation are published separately for each Standing Committee. Since 1919 sessional bound volumes of debates for each committee have appeared, with a separate index to every bill in each. There is no published general index to the Standing Committee debates for each session, but POLIS provides indexing in online form.

Bills and acts

Bills

One of the main functions of Parliament is to consider proposed legislation, mainly in the form of bills. These must pass through a complex series of stages allowing examination of their principles and detailed provisions.[3] Most bills are initiated by the government and almost all of these become law, but individual MPs can promote Private Members' Bills. Only a small proportion of these are enacted: in the 1989−90 session only 11 of the 126 Private Members' Bills became law. Examples include bills making poison pen letters illegal and requiring children to wear seat belts in the rear seats of cars. Both government and Private Members' Bills are Public Bills which, if passed, become law in one or more countries of the United Kingdom. Private Bills are a different category and come from promoters outside Parliament. They are usually put forward by local authorities, companies, and educational or charitable bodies which are seeking special powers applicable only to them. Proposed changes to Private Bill procedure will reduce their number as transport and harbour schemes will be dealt with by delegated legislation. Very occasionally Private Bills relate to an individual: historically they were used to obtain divorces or naturalize aliens.

Each bill must pass through three readings in each House. The majority commence in the Commons, but less controversial bills may start in the Lords. The first reading is a formality announcing the existence of the bill, after which it is printed. Bills are drafted in legal terminology and their purpose and effect may not be easily understood by the lay person. Many bills have a brief 'Explanatory memorandum' setting out their main proposals in simpler language, with their financial implications if they involve expenditure.

At second reading the principles behind the bill are examined and debated and the House votes on whether to accept or reject the bill. This is recorded in *Hansard*, of course. Uncontroversial bills may be referred to a Second Reading Committee in the Commons whose deliberations are reported separately in the Standing Committee debates. If the bill successfully passes its second reading the Speaker normally allocates it to a Standing Committee for detailed consideration of its clauses. General Standing Committees are referred to by letter; they consist of between 16 and 50 MPs (most have no more than 20 members), their membership changing with each new bill assigned to them. Private Members' Bills are considered only by Standing Committee C. Bills relating exclusively to Scotland, Wales or Northern Ireland go to committees composed predominantly of MPs from the relevant country.

A Standing Committee normally holds several sittings to examine a bill, the full record of each day's debates appearing in Standing

Committee debates. Summaries of the Standing Committee's proceedings and decisions are published separately as *Minutes of proceedings* in the House of Commons papers (q.v.). The chairman of the committee reports to the House of Commons on their consideration of the bill and any proposed amendments to it at Report Stage. The text of the bill is reprinted as amended in Standing Committee. The third reading in which the bill is reviewed by the House in its final form may follow directly after the Report Stage or may be taken days or weeks later.

If the Commons votes to approve the bill it is sent to the Lords where it goes through similar stages, except that the committee stage is normally taken before the whole House. The House of Lords may amend the bill, these amendments being printed separately in the House of Lords bills series. When the whole bill is reprinted with amendments it is given a new number, so one bill may have several different numbers during its progress through each House. If the Lords' amendments are approved at third reading the bill must be returned to the Commons for their agreement to the amendments.

Once the bill has been passed by both Houses it receives Royal Assent and becomes an Act of Parliament. The whole process normally takes several months and the passage of the bill must be completed within the one parliamentary session or it will lapse. Many bills are introduced in a session but far fewer become acts as some are rejected and others fail to complete all their stages. The *Weekly information bulletin* is the essential guide to the progress of any current bill.

Private bills are published by their promoter and are available from their Parliamentary Agents, not from HMSO. They go through similar stages in both Houses, but if there is opposition to the bill the committee stage is a public hearing at which objections can be put forward.

Acts

Once a bill has received Royal Assent it becomes an Act of Parliament and is published separately, though its provisions may not come into force immediately. Acts are cited by their short title, date and chapter number, e.g. Official Secrets Act 1989 c.6. Acts prior to 1963 may also include the regnal year in their citation e.g. Copyright Act 1956, 4 & 5 Eliz.2 c.74.

All the acts of a year are collected in the annual volumes of *Public General Acts and Measures*, with the exception of Local Acts. *Public General Acts and Measures* is issued by HMSO as a non-parliamentary publication, like the rest of the titles discussed in this section. The

Measures in its title are the General Synod Measures of the Church of England which also require Royal Assent, but relate only to church matters. Local Acts result from successful private bills. They are published separately by HMSO on receiving Royal Assent but are not issued in an annual collection. A list of them is included in *Public General Acts and Measures* and a separate list and index is published annually by HMSO: *The Local and Personal Acts: tables and index*. A cumulated *Index to Local and Personal Acts ... 1801 – 1947* (HMSO, 1949) and a continuation volume covering 1948 to 1966 group all such acts by their subject. They are cited differently: Local Acts have their chapter number in roman numerals, e.g. Avon Light Rail Transit Act 1989 c.iv, while for Personal Acts it is in italics.

An act adds to the existing body of the law in the UK and usually affects previous acts by amending their provisions or repealing them completely. Details of the acts affected and the changes made are listed in the schedules accompanying each new act and also in the tables appended to *Public General Acts and Measures*. The law can also be changed by statutory instruments and regulations issued by government departments (q.v.) and by judges' decisions on individual cases in the courts which are recorded in the law reports.

Because an act affects existing legislation and will itself be amended by subsequent legislation it is not sufficient simply to have its original text. Users need to be able to find out whether its provisions are still wholly or partly in force. The official collection of acts as amended by later legislation is *Statutes in force*. This is a series of over 100 looseleaf binders with Acts arranged in subject groups such as education, property, road traffic or sale of goods. Amended texts of Acts are published as separate booklets to be filed in the appropriate volume and replaced when there is further major amendment. Cumulative supplements for each subject group record more minor amendments and list new Acts on the topic.

Complementing *Statutes in force* are two annual works providing access to legislation by date and subject. The *Chronological table of the statutes in force* (2 vols) lists all acts since 1235 showing which are still wholly or partly in force. The *Index to the statutes in force* (2 vols) is an alphabetical subject index allowing acts on any topic to be traced. The subject headings have many subdivisions and cross references: to find legislation on noise you are referred to a subheading of 'Pollution'.

Many libraries prefer to stock commercially published editions of the acts like *Halsbury's statutes of England* (4th ed., Butterworths, 1985-).

This collects together the in-force legislation under subjects with a detailed general index and useful annotations to each Act. It is updated by the looseleaf *Current statutes service* for the most recent Acts. Legal databases like LEXIS also provide the full text of legislation: it includes all UK statutes and statutory instruments currently in force and is updated with new legislation. It also contains the law reports with details of all cases affecting the interpretation of the law. The Lord Chancellor's Department is considering producing its own legislative database of statutes in force. POLIS provides bibliographical references to all Public General Acts since 1979, and Local and Personal Acts and statutory instruments since 1982.

House of Commons Papers

This is a mixed group of papers which are required by the House under the provisions of an act (Act Papers) or by direction of the House (Returns) or which arise from the work of its committees. They are protected by parliamentary privilege and may contain statements which could not be included in a Command Paper or a non-parliamentary publication. The vast majority are the reports and evidence of select committees or the minutes of proceedings of standing committees considering legislation. The group also includes annual reports and/or accounts of many official bodies, financial papers, reports of investigations by the National Audit Office and by the Parliamentary Commissioners (Ombudsmen) as well as a few miscellaneous papers.

Each House of Commons Paper (HCP) is numbered at the foot of the cover and this should be included in any citation, together with the date of the session: e.g. *Report of Her Majesty's Chief Inspector of Prisons 1989* (HC 598, 1989−90). Not all of the papers laid before the House are published: over 700 papers were laid in the 1987−88 session and about 75% of these were published by HMSO. POLIS includes details of papers laid but not printed, and a full list can be found in the index to the House of Commons *Journal*.

Select Committee papers

Select committees are set up by the House of Commons to investigate and report back on various aspects of government activity. Different select committees examine the work of government departments, the Parliamentary Commissioners for Administration, statutory instruments, European legislation and matters relating to the House. They provide a means of highlighting a topic and investigating it on behalf of Parliament and in so doing they inform a wider public.

Select committees have a long and distinguished history, being responsible for many of the major investigations of the 19th century. The select committee system was revitalized in 1979 after a period when they had been overshadowed by other investigative bodies. The range of committees was revised and their powers of obtaining information increased. Fourteen departmental select committees were set up to examine the policy, administration and expenditure of the main government departments and their associated bodies. The Treasury and Civil Service Committee, for instance, examines the Treasury's economic forecasts and its administration of the economy. The effectiveness of these committees varies but they are a much better means of keeping watch on government activities than Question Time.

Other select committees deal with matters affecting the House like its accommodation, library services, procedure and MPs' interests. The powerful Committee of Public Accounts examines the audited accounts of government departments and associated bodies to detect waste and to ensure that expenditure sanctioned by the House has been properly accounted for. It issues a large number of reports each session (44 in 1989−90) on topics like *Quality control of road and bridge construction* (HC 174, 1989−90) and the use of operating theatres in the National Health Service. The Select Committee on European legislation examines European Community's draft proposals for legislation and reports to the House. Each of its reports deals with a number of proposals: the *31st report, session 1989−90* (HC 11 − xxxi) included such assorted topics as the advertising of tobacco products, aid to Eastern Europe, trade statistics and value added tax.[4]

Most departmental select committees consist of 11 MPs chosen according to party strength in the Commons, but their reports often transcend party divisions. They are appointed for the whole life of a Parliament rather than being disbanded at the end of each session. The departmental select committees usually recruit research assistants and specialist advisers to assist their monitoring of the department. The committees are advisory: they investigate a topic, take written statements and hear oral evidence before reporting back to the House with recommendations. Their reports may lead to government action on the topic.

Publications from the select committees all appear as House of Commons Papers. They include *Minutes of evidence* for each sitting at which witnesses are called, memoranda laid before the committee, the

Minutes of proceedings of each committee for the session, and the final report to the House on each topic investigated. A single investigation may produce a substantial volume of papers, all bearing the same paper number. The papers of the Social Services Committee on *Resourcing the National Health Service* (HC 264, 1987–88) include 12 volumes of minutes of evidence and four volumes of the final report. The latter contains the committee's conclusions together with minutes of the evidence heard and written evidence laid before the committee. The government will normally reply to the committee's observations in one of four ways: in a memorandum published as a HCP in a special report of the committee; in a policy statement published as a Command Paper; in a letter to the chairman; or occasionally in a statement in the House. Each select committee normally publishes several reports per session: the Energy Committee published seven reports in 1989-90 while the Social Services Committee produced 11.

There are several joint committees of the Lords and Commons dealing mainly with legislative matters. They report to both Houses and their papers are numbered in both the HCP and the House of Lords Papers series. The major committee is the Joint Committee on Statutory Instruments which draws the attention of both Houses to any SIs which are unusual in their provisions. It issued 28 reports in the 1989–90 session. The Joint Committee on Consolidation Bills takes the committee stage of bills consolidating all previous legislation on a topic into a single bill which removes duplication and inconsistencies but adds nothing new to the law. Other joint committees include the Ecclesiastical Committee which deals with Church of England Measures and the Joint Committee on Private Bill Procedure.

Reports of investigations

Apart from the investigations carried out by the various select committees, the House of Commons has officials responsible for the examination of public expenditure and investigation of complaints. The National Audit Office is headed by the Comptroller and Auditor General who is responsible to the House for certifying the accounts of all government departments and many other public bodies (the appropriation accounts). He can also investigate the economy and efficiency of the use of resources by these bodies and presents numerous reports to the House (31 in 1989). His reports are examined by the Public Accounts Committee and may be critical of policies and practices such as the undervaluing of property assets in privatizing the Royal Ordnance factories. There is a separate

31

Northern Ireland Audit Office, the major reports of which are also HCPs.

The reports of the Parliamentary Commissioners appointed by the House to investigate complaints from the public about maladministration by government departments and in the National Health Service are published as HCPs. About 70% of the complaints are rejected by the Commissioner and the remainder are investigated. The Parliamentary Commissioner for Administration and the Health Service Commissioner act for England, Scotland and Wales and publish reports on selected cases. The Health Service Commissioner received over 750 complaints in 1988-89 and issued 139 reports. These were summarized in three reports appearing as HCPs (HC 103, 393 and 457, 1988–89). There is a separate Parliamentary Commissioner for Administration for Northern Ireland whose reports also appear as HCPs. The Parliamentary Commissioner for Administration Committee supervises the work of these Commissioners.

Minutes of proceedings of Standing Committees

The *Minutes of proceedings* of all standing committees examining individual bills and statutory instruments are published separately as HCPs for each piece of legislation. They record the attendance, amendments moved and results of votes on the provisions of the legislation.

Administrative reports/accounts

A substantial number of administrative reports, usually annual, of public bodies appear as HCPs. These provide Parliament with a means of overseeing the work of organizations it has created and to which it has delegated specific powers. Such reports are often required under the terms of the act setting up the body. Organizations reporting annually to Parliament include the Crown Prosecution Service, the Forestry Commission and the Historic Buildings Council for Scotland. Some reports cover a longer period like the report on *Consumer safety* (HC 673, 1987–88) from 1983 to 1988. In many cases only the organization's accounts are required by Parliament and the report is published separately, usually by the body itself.

Publication of annual reports is fragmented: they may appear as HCPs, Command Papers, non-parliamentary publications (HMSO) or as publications of the individual organization. Until 1990 there was no consistent way in which the annual reports of government departments appeared, and several did not even produce one. From 1991 annual reports of all government departments have been published as separate volumes in *The government's expenditure plans* ... (q.v.). Englefield provides a list of reports published as HCPs and Command Papers, but many others no longer appear in these series.[1] Some recently established organizations are required to submit reports to the House, however, such as the *Ofgas annual report* from the Director General of Gas Supply and the first annual report of the Serious Fraud Office (HC 485, 1988–89).

Financial papers

A distinct group of HCPs is concerned with government expenditure. This includes the *Supply estimates* for expenditure by government departments in the coming financial year (in separate parts for each department); the supplementary estimates for the current financial year; and the appropriation accounts which cover actual expenditure in the previous financial year. The most important is the *Financial statement and budget report* by the Chancellor of the Exchequer in Spring. The *Autumn statement*, which outlines economic prospects and public spending plans for the coming year, was published as a HCP until the 1987–88 session but became a Command Paper in 1989.

Other reports and papers

The Law Commission and the Scottish Law Commission are permanent advisory bodies which review the law and recommend simplification or reform. The majority of their reports are published as HCPs like *Family law: the ground for divorce* (HC 636, 1989–90). Reports on consolidation of existing legislation (without change) appear as Command Papers, while the Law Commission consultation papers are HMSO non-parliamentary publications.

HCPs are also used to make particular information available to the House, like the occasional *Statement of changes in immigration rules* (e.g. HC 454, 1989–90) from the Home Office and the return of election expenses for candidates in general elections. Similarly the *Register of Members' interests* is published regularly to record the involvement of MPs in outside organizations so that potential conflicts of interest are clear.

House of Lords Papers

The House of Lords publishes substantially fewer papers than the Commons (under 100 in 1989–90). Until the 1986–87 session they were numbered in a single series of House of Lords Papers and Bills. The

Papers are now in a separate series with its own numbering. The prefix HL distinguishes them from House of Commons Papers in citations. The Lords has no standing committees for legislation but it has two important select committees for science and technology and the European Communities. Select committees on other topics are appointed as required, like the Select Committee on Murder and Life Imprisonment in the 1988−89 session. It also uses select committees to examine certain private bills and has others for procedure and the domestic functions of the House. The Select Committee on the European Communities is the parliamentary body which scrutinizes EC policies most thoroughly.[4] It has six subcommittees to examine proposals on aspects like agriculture and food or social and consumer affairs. It produces between 15 and 30 substantial reports a session on topics ranging from the integration of disabled people to relations with Japan. Reports include evidence taken from a wide range of witnesses though some are available in two versions, either with or without evidence.

Command Papers

Command Papers are a mixed group of government policy documents, treaties, investigative reports, annual reports and a few statistics. In quantitative terms fewer than half as many Command Papers as HCPs appear in a year (under 270 in 1988 and 343 in 1989). They are arguably of greater importance, however, as they deal with the policies the government intends to implement and the commitments which this country enters into, like the Single European Act. There have been changes in the relative significance of the different groups of Command Papers over the last decade as the number of Royal Commission and Committees of Inquiry reports has dwindled while government responses to select committee reports have become more common.

Command Papers are united by their method of publication, technically 'by Command of Her Majesty', which brings before Parliament papers produced outside the House. In practice the appropriate minister decides whether to present a paper to Parliament and political considerations apply, particularly with reports and policy documents. Unlike HCPs, the numbering of Command Papers does not begin afresh in each session. They are instead allocated a prefix, which is an abbreviation of Command, and a running number. A new series begins when the numbering approaches 10,000. The current series, which began in November 1986, is the sixth and has the prefix Cm. The first series began in 1833 with no prefix:

1833–69	1 to 4222
1870–99	C.1 to C.9550
1900–1918	Cd.1 to Cd.9239
1919–56	Cmd.1 to Cmd.9889
1956–86	Cmnd.1 to Cmnd.9927
1986–	Cm.1-

Since the numbering is not related to the parliamentary session guides are needed to locate Command Papers in the sessional volumes.[5]

Policy documents

Government policy documents form an important group within the Command Papers. There are two main kinds: consultative 'green papers' and 'white papers' which are definitive statements of the policy the government intends to put into effect. Green papers are published to promote public discussion of the topic and contain the government's preliminary thinking without committing it to a specific course of action. *Competition and choice: telecommunications policy for the 1990s* (Cm.1303, 1990) sets out government ideas on widening competition in telecommunications. After a period of consultation the government usually formulates its policy and issues a definitive statement. The three consultative papers on legal services in January 1989 brought over 2,000 responses from the legal profession and the public. The white paper on *Legal services: a framework for the future* (Cm.740) appeared in July 1989. It set out the government's decisions on the future legal system and analysed the responses to the green papers. A bill was introduced in the 1989–90 session and the Courts and Legal Services Act received Royal Assent in November 1990.

Definitive policy statements on important topics normally appear as Command Papers and are usually a warning of impending legislation, the main lines of which will be indicated in the white paper (as the example above shows). The policy statement may have been preceded by the report of an investigative committee on the topic. *Charities: a framework for the future* (Cm.694, 1989), for instance, shows how the government intends to implement the recommendations of the Woodfield report on the work of the Charity Commission in new legislation. *The government's expenditure plans* . . . (annual) reviews public expenditure for the forthcoming three years in detail, setting out the spending plans for each department in separate volumes, combined with the department's annual report from 1991. The *Autumn statement* became a Command

35

Paper in 1989 and is now the central document for the announcement of public expenditure plans. In a few cases a summary of a white paper will be issued. *This common inheritance: Britain's environmental strategy* (Cm.1200, 1990) ran to almost 300 pages, and a 36-page summary appeared as a non-parliamentary publication.

Not all white papers are Command Papers: policy statements on topics regarded as less important may be non-parliamentary publications or may be announced to the House and recorded in *Hansard*. Consultative papers on topics like financing the public library service, restrictive trade practices, *Punishment, custody and the community* (Cm.424, 1988) and *Summer time* (Cm.722, 1989) have appeared as Command Papers, but the great majority are published departmentally or by HMSO as non-parliamentary publications. Green and white papers are not always clearly identified as such in HMSO catalogues, but there is a regular list of those received each week in the *Weekly information bulletin*, including ones issued as non-parliamentary and non-HMSO publications.

Government policies are also defined in the growing number of government responses to select committee reports. These reports are often critical of the government and force it to set out its views on a range of controversial matters. This group now forms around 10% of all Command Papers. The responses are variously termed as reply, observations or comments on the reports, or Treasury minutes in the case of responses to the reports of the Public Accounts Committee. The reply may take several months: *The government's reply to the 2nd report from the Home Affairs Committee, session 1989–90, HC 92: compensating victims quickly* (Cm.1153, 1990) took the Home Office over six months to produce.

Treaties and agreements
Treaties, conventions and agreements with other countries and with international organizations make up about half of all Command Papers. They are the means by which MPs are informed of international obligations the government has entered into. Britain's role as a trading nation, its substantial overseas investments and its links with European and Commonwealth countries involve it in many treaties and agreements. These cover topics like trade, taxation and pensions, extradition of criminals, overflying rights, and cultural and economic cooperation. The procedures for parliamentary scrutiny of treaties are complex and are summarized in a Factsheet from the Public Information Office.[6]

These agreements are published in five series: the *Treaty series*, the 'country' series (not its official name), the *European Communities* series, the *Transport series*, and the *Miscellaneous series*. The *European Communities* series includes agreements between EC countries and other states, mainly on trade, and agreements between member states like the *Convention between member states of the European Communities on double jeopardy* (Cm.438, 1988). The *Treaty series* is the most numerous and includes the majority of agreements between the British government and foreign states.

Documents in all five series are brought together under the heading 'Treaties, etc' in the HMSO catalogues. Each series has its own numbering in addition to the Command number. Agreements printed in these series may not be operative immediately; a *Supplementary list of ratifications, accessions, withdrawals, etc.* is published regularly for those in the *Treaty series*. This series is also very well indexed with an annual index and, until 1979, a general index covering three to four years. There is a comprehensive chronological list of older treaties, with subject and country indexes, in *An index of British treaties 1101–1968* (3 vols., HMSO, 1970).

Investigative reports

Royal Commissions have traditionally been the most prestigious of the investigative bodies. They examined topics of public concern where legislation seemed desirable. In the 1970s they produced reports and recommendations on legal services, criminal procedure, gambling, the press and the National Health Service. No new Royal Commission was appointed between 1979 and 1990. The revitalized select committees fulfil part of their role, but the membership of Royal Commissions is not restricted to MPs and they can spend longer investigating a subject in depth. Rodgers provides an interesting insight into the appointment of a Royal Commission and details of their major investigations since 1946.[7]

Royal Commissions can receive written submissions and hear oral evidence from any individual or organization. They sometimes employ researchers to produce studies and background papers. A single Commission may issue a considerable number of publications, although normally only the main report and appendices appear as Command Papers. The final report is a substantial volume reviewing the whole issue and recommending action. A shorter version may be produced for a more general readership like *The balance of criminal justice* (1981) which summarized the report of the Royal Commission on Criminal Procedure (Cmnd.8092, 1981). Oral and written evidence, research studies and background papers may be published separately but are normally non-parliamentary publications. The Royal Commission on the Press (1975-77) produced an *Interim report* (Cmnd.6433, 1976), a two-volume *Final report* (Cmnd.6810, 1977), six papers in its *Research series* (in this case all as Command Papers) and four *Working papers*.

Most Royal Commissions are appointed for a specific task and disband once they have reported. A few standing Royal Commissions continue to report over many years. The oldest still reporting is the Royal Commission on Historical Manuscripts founded in 1869, but its reports are not now Command Papers. The Royal Commission on Environmental Pollution was appointed as a standing body in 1970 and issued its thirteenth report in 1989: *The release of genetically engineered organisms to the environment* (Cm.720). The government is not bound to accept the recommendations of a Royal Commission and may ignore or reverse them if it wishes.

Investigations may also be undertaken by individuals or committees appointed by a minister to report on a specific matter of concern to his department. The investigation is carried out within the terms of reference given when the inquiry is set up and these may limit its scope. The reports will be published as Command Papers or as non-parliamentary or non-HMSO publications depending on a political decision by the minister. *The Report of the inquiry into child abuse in Cleveland 1987* (Cm.412 and 413, 1988) by Elizabeth Butler-Sloss and the report of the review committee on *The parole system in England and Wales* (Cm.532, 1988) were both Command Papers while the *Report of the Beat the Cowboys Working Party* (1988) — which dealt with builders, not flagellation — was non-parliamentary. If these investigative bodies produce evidence or other papers separately from the report it may be hard to trace. Written evidence submitted by organizations may be available directly from them, either separately or in their journal. A list of departmental committees and working parties for the period 1900–1972 can be found in Pemberton.[8]

A number of standing investigative bodies report in the Command Papers series. The Monopolies and Mergers Commission investigates proposed takeovers which may not be in the public interest and cases where companies have such a large market share for their products that competition may be restricted.[9] It also investigates the performance of nationalized industries. Reports include *Thomson Travel Group and Horizon Travel Ltd: a report on the merger situation* (Cm.554, 1989) and *Welsh Water Authority: a report on the Authority's efficiency, costs and service* (Cm.366, 1988). Most but not all of its reports are Command Papers: *Chatlines and message services* (1989) was a non-parliamentary publication.

The reports of pay review bodies for a number of professions like the Review Body on Doctors' and Dentists' Remuneration and the Review Body on Top Salaries are Command Papers. Some reports of standing departmental advisory committees like the Industrial Injuries Advisory Council and the Social Security Advisory Committee appear as Command Papers, though most advisory bodies' publications are non-parliamentary or non-HMSO. On rare occasions a Tribunal of Inquiry will be set up to investigate and report on matters like breaches of security when no other method of investigation is considered adequate.

Administrative reports, statistics and other papers
Annual or regular reports like the *Annual report on Hong Kong* or the annual *Report of the Commissioners of Her Majesty's Inland Revenue* represent about 10% of Command Papers. This category has been reinforced by the reports of government departments which have appeared annually as separate volumes in *The government's expenditure plans ...* since 1991. As with HCPs, some new annual reports like the first *Annual report ... on the Social Fund* (Cm.748, 1989) are issued as Command Papers. An illustration of one of the apparent illogicalities of official publishing is the appearance of the annual *Report of the Commissioner of Police of the Metropolis ...* as a Command Paper while the *Report of Her Majesty's Chief Inspector of Constabulary* is a House of Commons Paper!

A few sets of annual statistics are published as Command Papers, though this is a declining group. They are mainly figures collected by the Home Office on prisons, crime, immigration, and experiments on animals together with the *Judicial statistics* from the Lord Chancellor's Department. Some of these are supplemented by Home Office statistical bulletins which are non-HMSO publications. Useful statistics can also be found in annual reports and some investigative reports like certain of the Monopolies and Mergers Commission reports.

A few other papers appear as Command Papers if the minister so decides. One of the most useful of these is the six-monthly summary of *Developments in the European Community* presented to Parliament by the Foreign Secretary. This is a way of keeping up to date with progress on EC proposals, measures implementing the Single European Market and meetings involving UK ministers.

Sessional Papers

The traditional method of arranging all of the papers produced by both Houses of Parliament in a session is to bind them in multi-volume sets of sessional papers. The House of Commons set contains all Public Bills, House of Commons Papers and Command Papers while the Lords set comprises HL Papers and HL Bills. A number of libraries have sets of the Commons sessional papers dating back to the beginning of the nineteenth century, but Lords sets are much rarer. This is unfortunate as they complement the Commons sessional papers for bills and contain some unique material such as the reports of the Lords Select Committee on the European Communities and some major reports of the nineteenth century.[10]

Several reprint editions of the Commons sessional papers have increased their availability. One of the most extensive is the Chadwyck-Healey microfiche collection of *House of Commons parliamentary papers*, which also saves a great deal of space. It reprints all the papers of the 19th century and the first half of the 20th (to 1960−61) and current papers since the 1975−76 session, with subject indexes. Chadwyck-Healey is now issuing papers covering the sessions from 1961−62 to 1974−75. Older papers are reprinted in the *House of Commons sessional papers of the eighteenth century*, edited and indexed by Sheila Lambert and published by Scholarly Resources (147 vols, 1975−76). Readex offers the House of Commons sessional papers from 1731 to the present, House of Lords sessional papers since 1940/41, Lords and Commons *Hansards*, and the *Journal of the House of Commons*. The collection is being reformatted to microfiche and will be complete in 1992. The extensive Irish University Press 1,000-volume edition of the nineteenth century sessional papers in subject groups is a useful printed collection, though it is selective. The House of Lords sessional papers have been reprinted by Oceana (1972−78) in printed form for 1641−1805 and in microfilm for 1806−59. Current HL Papers from the 1984−85 session are available on microfiche from Chadwyck-Healey. The number of reprint editions emphasizes the great value of the parliamentary papers to historians of all kinds. They are major primary sources not only for all aspects of the history of Britain but for its many former colonies as well.

The traditional arrangement of the sessional papers hinders an approach by subject. From 1800 to the 1968−69 session bills, reports of Commons committees, reports of commissioners and accounts and papers were arranged in four separate groups. This split reports and legislation on the same topic, though different versions of the same bill were kept together. This arrangement was modified for the ten years from 1969—70 to 1978—79, and changed to the current arrangement of bills, House of Commons Papers and Command Papers each in their own numerical sequence from 1979—80. It is now easy to refer to a specific paper if the number is known, but indexes and guides are still needed to find all the material on a particular topic.

Official sessional indexes have been compiled since 1800 to make papers accessible. This is especially useful up to 1979 since it is not possible to refer directly to an individual paper unless its session and number and the volume and page within the sessional set are known. Indexes list papers by number, by subject and by name of chairman or author. Subject headings are fairly consistent but familiarity with them improves the retrieval of relevant papers. The sessional indexes are cumulated into decennial and general indexes for the Commons, the latter covering about 50 years. Each general index (1800—52, 1852/53—99 and 1900—1949) varies in quality of indexing and ease of use. Recent sessional indexes since 1979 use the POLIS thesaurus for subject headings but are slow to appear: the 1983—84 Commons index was published in 1988. Lords indexes are cumulated only for 1800—59, 1860—70 and 1871—85, after which sessional indexes must be used up to 1920, since when no indexes have been published. The POLIS database offers a more up to date alternative to the printed indexes from 1979 for the Commons sessional papers and covers Lords Papers and Bills from November 1981.

Indexes and guides to sessional papers have also been prepared by other publishers to ease the task of the researcher.[11] The Ford breviates and select lists (discussed in Chapter 5) provide a means of tracing the main sessional papers since 1833. Earlier papers can be found through the *Catalogue of parliamentary reports and a breviate of their contents ... 1696—1834* (Hansard's catalogue), first published in 1834, and Sheila Lambert's index to the 18th century sessional papers (1715—99) in the Scholarly Resources reprint. The whole of the 19th century is covered in the *Subject catalogue of the House of Commons Parliamentary Papers 1801—1900* (5 vols, Chadwyck-Healey, 1988). This brings together all papers on the same subject and gives the microfiche number of each in the Chadwyck-Healey reprint. The same publisher is producing a cumulating microfiche *Monthly index to the House of Commons Parliamentary Papers* for papers in the current session and indexes for sessions since 1985—86 which appear long before the official printed indexes.

The Parliamentary On Line Information Service (POLIS)
The House of Commons Library introduced the POLIS online database in 1980 to replace its range of manual indexes.[12] It is designed specifically to serve MPs but approved organizations outside Parliament can access it on a subscription basis. A change of host in 1988 from Scicon to UCC resulted in higher charges which reduced the number of external users. POLIS is potentially a powerful tool for the researcher in easing access to official information. It is a citation database which provides detailed indexing of parliamentary questions, ministerial statements, debates, bills, House of Commons and House of Lords Papers, Command Papers and selected non-parliamentary, non-HMSO and European Community publications. Coverage starts from varying dates between 1979 and 1984. Each individual question, statement, debate or publication has its own record which includes date and source information, the government department or MP involved, any relevant legislation, subject index terms from the POLIS thesaurus and other terms which identify the topic. These elements allow several different approaches to the item when searching. If required, searches can be restricted to a specific type of record, e.g. written questions, Command Papers, or to wider groups of material, e.g. parliamentary questions, parliamentary papers. Printed sources (or *Hansard* and statutory instruments on CD-ROM) must be used to obtain the full text of the items retrieved.

POLIS is updated on a daily basis, with a delay of between one day and two weeks, so it is quite current. Its advantages lie in the immediate availability of the information, the detailed subject and name indexing, and the ability to cover several years in a single search (or to limit to a specific date). It is particularly useful for access to questions because of the large number answered each session and the valuable information they contain. Considerable familiarity with official publications and parliamentary procedure is needed to exploit it effectively, however. Libraries wishing to become users must send staff on an expensive training course. Changes to the software in 1989 simplified searching, and the database can be approached through menus based on the types of document sought. There is a monthly charge as well as connect time charges for actual use. The occasional user would be better advised to approach the House of Commons Public Information Office for help. The POLIS thesaurus has been used in the preparation of the fortnightly index to *Hansard* and recent sessional indexes.

Computerization makes it easier to analyse and repackage large quantities of data. Campaign Information launched its regularly updated

Parliamentary analysis in 1988 with details of the voting record of individual MPs in every House of Commons division. It also produces special reports like *Conservative dissent* (1989) which analysed voting by Conservative MPs against the government. This information is useful to those lobbying MPs and seeking to influence the government.

References and further reading

1   A more detailed analysis of the work of Parliament and of the information it obtains from government can be found in: Englefield, D., *Whitehall and Westminster*, Longman, 1985. The work of Parliament and its procedure are explained in a number of books, e.g. Silk, P. and Walters, R., *How Parliament works*, Longman, 1987; Davis, D., *The BBC viewer's guide to Parliament*, BBC Books, 1989.

2   Holden, H., 'Production of the printed indexes to the House of Commons official report', *State librarian*, **35** (3), November 1987, 37−9.

3   Millar, D., 'Bills from the inside', *Refer*, **4** (4), Autumn 1987, 6−10.

4   Englefield, D., 'Parliament and the European Communities' in *Brussels: Whitehall: Westminster: proceedings of a one-day seminar on British and European official publishing* ... edited by Valerie J. Nurcombe, Library Association, Information Services Group, SCOOP, 1989, 26−32.

5   Di Roma, E. and Rosenthal, J., *A numerical finding list of British Command Papers published 1833−1961/62*, New York Public Library, 1967; McBride, E. A., *British Command Papers: a numerical finding list 1962/63−1976/77*, Atlanta, Georgia, Emory University, 1982.

6   Ware, R., *Treaties and the House of Commons*, House of Commons Public Information Office, 1990. (Factsheet 57).

7   Rodgers, F., *A guide to British government publications*, New York, H. W. Wilson, 1980, 165−6.

8   Pemberton, J. E., *British official publications*, 2nd ed., Pergamon Press, 1973, 162−94.

9   Monopolies and Mergers Commission, *The role of the Commission*, 3rd ed., HMSO, 1990.

10 Mallaber, K., 'The House of Lords sessional papers', *Journal of librarianship*, **4** (2), April 1972, 106−14.

11 Bond, M. F., *Guide to the records of Parliament*, HMSO, 1971; Cockton, P., *House of Commons parliamentary papers 1801–1900. Guide to the Chadwyck-Healey microfiche edition*, Chadwyck-Healey, (forthcoming); Ford, P. and Ford, G., *A guide to parliamentary papers*, 3rd ed., Irish University Press, 1972.
12 Englefield, D., *Whitehall and Westminster*, Longman, 1985, 132–41; Siswell, A., 'POLIS: the parliamentary online information system', *Law librarian*, **17** (1), April 1986, 23–6; Southgate, M. and Wainwright, J., 'POLIS' in *British official publications online* edited by Valerie J. Nurcombe, Library Association, Information Services Group, SCOOP, 1990, 16–24.

3 Government department publishing

While HMSO has a virtual monopoly of publishing on behalf of Parliament, government departments publish a large amount of material themselves. HMSO restricts itself mainly to statutory publications and material from government departments which will produce a sufficient financial return. These form the bulk of its non-parliamentary publications. The remainder are publications of other British official bodies issued through HMSO (discussed in Chapter 4). Few writers on official publications have done justice to the range of publications from government departments, both HMSO and those directly published by the department, though Rodgers provides an extensive survey.[1] In this chapter a brief examination of the range and duties of government departments is followed by an analysis of the main types of HMSO non-parliamentary publications and a summary of publishing by government departments themselves.

GOVERNMENT DEPARTMENTS

Government departments have been created or extended in scope as the government has involved itself in more and more aspects of national life. The modern departmental structure began to emerge in the late 18th century with the assignment of responsibility for Home Affairs and Foreign Affairs to two Secretaries of State. The system developed fully in the 20th century with the creation of a comprehensive range of government departments for health, social security, employment, transport, energy and the environment. The 1960s brought a trend to umbrella departments created from the merger of two or more ministries to form, for instance, the Ministry of Defence or the Department of the Environment. There has since been some retreat from the idea that biggest is administratively best with the separation of the Departments of Health and Social Security and the removal of the Department of Transport from the Department of the Environment.

The organization of the machinery of government is not static and each government makes its own changes. These may be less dramatic than the creation of new departments. In 1985, for instance, responsibility for small firms and tourism shifted from the Department of Trade and Industry to the Department of Employment. More major changes have resulted from the report of the Prime Minister's Efficiency Unit on *Improving management in government: the next steps* (1988) which recommended the creation of a series of new executive agencies through hiving-off parts of government departments. The Department of Transport's Vehicle Inspectorate and HMSO itself were among the first agencies designated under this new initiative which aims to reduce government departments to a much smaller core of staff concerned with policy matters. By mid-1991 a total of 51 services employing over 210,000 staff (a third of the total Civil Service strength) had been established as executive agencies. They range from the National Weights and Measures Laboratory with 50 staf to the Social Security Benefits Agency with 68,000. The strategic control of these agencies remains with the appropriate minister, but a Chief Executive is responsible for day to day operations. Changes in the structure of government create difficulties when searching for publications, especially over a long period.

Ministers and civil servants

Government departments are staffed by civil servants and the major departments range in size from under 10,000 (Department of Health) to around 120,000 staff (Ministry of Defence). A government minister is the political head of each department answerable to Parliament for all its actions. The minister, usually titled Secretary of State, may be assisted by a Minister of State if the department has a heavy or wide-ranging workload: a Minister of State takes charge of housing and planning in the Department of the Environment, for instance. Most departments have junior ministers (Parliamentary Under Secretaries of State, or 'Pussy' to civil servants) to assist the departmental minister. The departmental minister makes the final decisions on matters of policy affecting the department, in consultation with colleagues in the Cabinet for important matters. Permanent civil servants are responsible for administering the government's policies.

The central offices of most government departments are in London, but several departments have regional offices throughout the country. A few, such as the Department of Social Security or the Department of Employment, have local offices in most towns. Some of the functions of government departments have been delegated to executive bodies specially created for the purpose, like the Health and Safety Commission and Executive.

Range of departments

There is little space here to reveal the complex web of government involvement in almost every aspect of British life.[2] The latest edition of *Britain: an official handbook* discusses the functions of government departments more fully than this brief review. The Treasury has always been a key department: the Prime Minister is traditionally the First Lord of the Treasury. The Chancellor of the Exchequer is the chief Treasury minister and the department is responsible for national economic strategy. Its control of government departments and their programmes is strong in financial terms, and it is jointly responsible with the Cabinet Office for control of the Civil Service. The Foreign and Commonwealth Office deals with relations with other countries and maintains embassies and high commissions abroad. The Overseas Development Administration is responsible for financial and technical aid to other countries. The Home Office has an assortment of responsibilities for most aspects of law and order, community relations and immigration, regulation of broadcasting, and control of drugs and firearms. Much of its work is carried out through inspectorates for the Probation Service, the Constabulary or the Fire Service.

A range of functional departments administer government policy in particular fields. The broad responsibilities of the Ministry of Agriculture, Fisheries and Food are clear from its title. The Ministry of Defence deals with defence policy and controls the armed forces. The Department of Education and Science is responsible for education at all levels and for civil science. The Department of Employment is concerned with employment and training policy and legislation, health and safety at work, and small firms. The Department of Energy has overall responsibility for policies relating to all forms of energy and energy conservation, and relations with the energy industries. The Department of the Environment looks after planning, housing policy, local government, sport and recreation, and a wide range of other environmental matters. The Department of Health oversees the National Health Service and personal social services while the Department of Social Security administers the social security system. The Office of Population Censuses and Surveys administers the registration of births, deaths and marriages, compiles population and health statistics and carries out surveys on behalf of other government departments. The Department of Trade and Industry has wide-ranging responsibilities for industrial and commercial policy, including competition policy, encouragement of exports, and consumer protection. The Department of Transport administers all aspects of transport policy: civil aviation, merchant shipping, rail transport, and the planning and maintenance of motorways and trunk roads.

The major government departments, each headed by a minister who is usually a member of Cabinet, are well known. There are also smaller departments carrying out specialized functions which are headed by civil servants. These include the Crown Prosecution Service, the Office of Gas Supply and the Board of Inland Revenue. A minister is responsible to Parliament for each of these departments, but will have other duties as well: the minister answerable for the Inland Revenue is also a Minister of State at the Treasury.

The geographical area for which government departments administer policy varies. Some departments, like the Foreign and Commonwealth Office, cover the United Kingdom as a whole, but others are restricted to Great Britain, or England and Wales, or England only. The Welsh Office is responsible for many aspects of policy and administration for Wales. Consequently a large number of publications are issued jointly by a government department responsible for England and the Welsh Office. Scotland has even greater devolution of administration with a Secretary of State for Scotland and five main government departments administering policy for agriculture and fisheries, development, education, industry, and home and health matters. These are known collectively as the Scottish Office. Central government departments work closely with the Scottish Office when exercising responsibilities for Scotland. Northern Ireland is currently ruled directly from Westminster through the Secretary of State for Northern Ireland who controls the six Northern Ireland departments.

The publications of government departments, their branches, divisions and units are discussed in this chapter. Organizations which have distinctive and specialized functions, like the Patent Office or the Ordnance Survey, many of which are now or will become executive agencies, are dealt with in the next chapter on national and regional public bodies.

HMSO PUBLISHING FOR GOVERNMENT DEPARTMENTS

Virtually all government departments issue some publications to inform Parliament and the public of their activities and policies or to make available information they have collected or produced. The output of one or two departments is mainly parliamentary: the majority of Foreign and Commonwealth Office publications are treaties appearing as Command Papers. But other departments issue much more as non-parliamentary publications through HMSO or as direct publications not published by or available from HMSO. The range of material published by HMSO on behalf of government departments is extensive, even though HMSO's share of departmental publishing is declining. In 1987 and 1988 around 1,300 titles appeared as non-parliamentary publications (excluding delegated legislation). Table 3 shows in outline the range and diversity of non-parliamentary publications. These categories are not mutually exclusive and there is inevitably some overlap.

Table 3   Types of HMSO publications from government departments

Legislation:	Advice and guidance:
Statute law collections	Advisory publications
Delegated legislation	Training materials
	Codes of practice and guidelines
Circulars, memoranda and	
case reports	Reference sources
Reports:	
Administrative	Periodicals
Enquiry and advisory	
Technical and research	Statistics and surveys
Policy papers	Historical, archaeological and
	cultural publications
	Bibliographic and research sources

Legislation

Statute law collections
Individual bills and acts are parliamentary publications but the collected acts in *Public General Acts and Measures* and *Statutes in force* together with the indexes and lists of legislation discussed in Chapter 2 are non-parliamentary publications from the Statutory Publications Office. Some

government departments issue the collected texts of relevant legislation through HMSO, notably *The law relating to social security* (1988, 10 vols with looseleaf updating) from the Department of Social Security and *The taxes acts* (5 vols, annual) from the Board of Inland Revenue. Commercially published collections of legislation covering specific topics are also available, many in looseleaf format for ease of updating, like the *Encyclopaedia of road traffic law and practice* from Sweet and Maxwell. The LEXIS full-text online service covers current public general acts and general statutory instruments as well as reports of cases among its databases.

Delegated legislation

Delegated legislation is by far the largest single category of non-parliamentary publications. It consists of administrative regulations and orders made by government departments and other public bodies under powers delegated to them by Parliament. This allows Parliament to concentrate on the principles of legislation in acts, leaving the details to ministers. Statutory instruments are the best known form of delegated legislation, over 2,000 of which are issued each year. There is parliamentary control of delegated legislation through a joint committee of both Houses of Parliament, a Commons Select Committee on Statutory Instruments and Commons Standing Committees, the last examining many individual statutory instruments.

Statutory instruments (SIs) appear on many topics including the road vehicle construction and use regulations, health and safety regulations, building regulations, routes of motorways and alterations to trunk roads, and social security regulations. They may also be used to bring into force an act or a section of an act. Most statutory instruments of general applicability are published individually, but HMSO has no obligation to publish those relating to a particular locality, only some of which are printed. Most SIs relating to local speed limits and traffic restrictions are unpublished, except on lamp-posts and in local newspapers. In 1989, for instance, over 1,200 local SIs were made, only 22% of which were printed. A *Table of local instruments* listing all those made since 1922 is being compiled by the Statutory Publications Office, but is unlikely to appear for some time. The easiest way for the public to gain access to local SIs is through the microfiche set held by the British Library Official Publications and Social Sciences Service, though at present they have been filmed only to 1981.

Each statutory instrument has a number which must be cited for precise identification, e.g. SI 1990 No.1791 *The Home energy efficiency grants regulations 1990*. Collected annual volumes of statutory instruments are published with the text of each general instrument still in force in full and a list of the local instruments, but take over two years to appear. One of the most current sources for collected statutory instruments is *SI-CD: Statutory Instruments on CD-ROM*, jointly published by HMSO and Context Ltd. It contains the full text of all published statutory instruments since January 1987 and is updated twice a year. It is searchable by any word or combination of words in the text, giving access to all relevant SIs.

The first official notice of the existence of a statutory instrument is the issue list in the *Daily list* of government publications which gives full details including the date of commencement. There is a separate monthly *List of statutory instruments* which records them by broad subject groups whether or not they have been published. This cumulates into an annual list by subject with numerical and alphabetical subject indexes. Both sources include a separate list of Northern Ireland statutory rules (since 1983).

As with acts, it is essential to be able to trace those statutory instruments still in force. No complete official collection of those in force is available. The most convenient source is the LEXIS full-text database of all SIs currently in force. Current statutory instruments on a few topics are issued with explanatory notes like *The building regulations 1985* (2nd ed., 1990). The two guides to statutory instruments in force are essential though both appear long after the date at which instruments were in force. The *Index to government orders in force*, which is published every two years, provides a subject approach. It identifies the acts under which statutory instruments may be made, the powers granted, and the titles of any relevant statutory instruments. The annual *Table of government orders* is a chronological list of general statutory instruments clearly identifying those still in force. Many libraries provide a commercial edition, *Halsbury's statutory instruments* (Butterworths, 24 vols, 1986–), which collects into subject groups the texts of the more important statutory instruments in force and provides regular supplements for newly published instruments.

Apart from statutory instruments delegated legislation includes Orders in (Privy) Council and Royal Instruments and Proclamations. Most of these are published in the annual collection of SIs but some appear only in the *London gazette* (q.v.). Legislation for Northern Ireland since 1972, when direct rule from Westminster was introduced, has been by Orders in Council. Government departments may publish regulations through HMSO. The *Queen's regulations* for each of the armed forces are constantly updated looseleaf publications covering every aspect of service life.

Circulars, memoranda and case reports

Not all government policy requires delegated legislation to bring it into effect. Acts may provide sufficient powers, leaving the detailed implementation to the minister. In such cases departmental circulars are used to announce government policy and to explain how it is to be put into effect. The Department of the Environment circular 1988/20 lays down the *Code of recommended practice on local authority publicity* to prevent politically-inspired advertising campaigns. Each circular is numbered and dated, as this example shows. Individual circulars from the Department of the Environment and the Department of Transport are published and sold through HMSO but many others are non-HMSO publications distributed to the local authorities or other bodies concerned. One department which collects its circulars into annual volumes, together with the administrative memoranda announcing changes in administrative procedure, is the Department of Education and Science in *Circulars and administrative memoranda issued*. Several departments use memoranda for administrative or technical matters like the Department of Health Technical Memorandum 82 *Firecode: alarm and detection systems* (1989).

HMSO publishes the reports and decisions on cases heard by several important tribunals. These are quasi-judicial bodies set up to deal with certain kinds of disputes; their work is discussed at the end of the next chapter. Cases are normally reported in collected volumes as with the *Value Added Tax Tribunals reports* (annually in four parts), or the Immigration Appeal Tribunal's *Immigration appeals* (quarterly). The decisions of commissioners in social security benefits cases are published separately for each type of benefit, and digests of the decisions are collected in the looseleaf publication *Social security case law*. Individual tax cases which are the subject of appeals to the High Court are published separately but are available only on annual subscription.

Reports

Reports of various kinds form a major portion of HMSO non-parliamentary publications whether they summarize the activities of an official organization, offer advice to a minister or contain the results of technical or research studies.

Administrative reports

Administrative reports form a distinct category providing regular summaries of the work of official bodies. The main text of the report is supported by statistics and financial accounts for the period in many cases. Reports are usually published annually, but some appear at other frequencies or irregularly. The different ways in which they may be published were referred to in Chapter 2. Reports appearing as non-parliamentary publications include *On the state of the public health*, *Her Majesty's Inspectorate of Pollution report*, *Railway safety* (an annual report from the Department of Transport's Railway Inspectorate), and the *Audit Commission report and accounts*.

Enquiry and advisory reports

A large number of enquiry and advisory reports are published as non-parliamentary publications, unless the minister decides that the report should be presented to Parliament. They include the reports of individuals, committees of enquiry or working parties appointed by the appropriate minister to investigate and report on a topic of concern. The *Report of the Committee of Enquiry into the teaching of English language* (1988) is the result of an inquiry set up by the Secretary of State for Education and Science to examine the way English is taught in schools. It recommends and discusses the range of skills needed. Like the equivalent parliamentary reports these are usually referred to by the name of the individual investigator or chairman, in this case John Kingman. The committee normally takes a considerable time over its deliberations: a Committee of Enquiry was set up by the Secretary of State for the Environment in April 1985 to advise on the future handling of geographic information. Its report appeared relatively quickly in May 1987. A committee's recommendations may form the basis for subsequent government policy or may be ignored. The evidence and submissions to these committees are not normally published by HMSO, except for Royal Commissions, but must be sought from the organization submitting the evidence.

Once enquiries have been completed the committee is disbanded, but there are also many standing organizations providing continuing advice and reports to the government. Quite a number of these reports are issued by HMSO. The Audit Commission undertakes studies to improve the economy, efficiency and effectiveness of local authorities and issues reports like *Assuring quality in education* (1989) and *The administration of the community charge* (1990). Reports of several other advisory bodies like the Library and Information Services Council are published by HMSO, sometimes in series such as the *Library information series*, e.g. 18. *Keys to success: performance indicators for public libraries* (1990). The work of other advisory bodies is discussed in Chapter 4. Enquiry and advisory reports are often of considerable importance to practitioners and students in the field and may have a long-term value whether or not the government of the day acted on them.

Technical and research reports

Technical and research reports are usually of most interest to specialists, though some are on issues of wider public concern. The Home Office Research and Planning Unit, for instance, has produced a considerable number of important and often controversial research studies including *Drinking and disorder* (No. 108, 1989) and *Electronic monitoring* (No. 120, 1990). The Cabinet Office's *Annual review of government funded R & D* regularly examines the whole range of government supported research. Many technical studies and research reports are published directly by government departments or research organizations. HMSO publishes a smaller proportion of this kind of material, generally those with policy implications or a fairly wide potential readership. The majority of government departments have some publications of this nature. The most extensive is the Department of Energy's *Offshore technology reports* series which presents results of projects funded by the Department and major companies, like *Helicopter rescue from offshore survival craft* (OTH 90 319, 1990). The Department of Social Security's research reports include *Tipping the balance: a study of non-take up of benefits in an inner city area* (1988) which is of interest to social workers and advisers as well as to the government. The Department of Transport has published a number of technical studies such as a survey of *The performance of concrete in bridges* (1989). Research and technical studies may be commissioned by government departments from outside consultants: the *M25 review* (2 vols, 1989) was carried out by Rendel Palmer & Tritton and Traffic Planning Associates, while Coopers and Lybrand Deloitte reported on *CFCs and halons: alternatives and the scope for recovery for recycling and destruction* (1990) for the Department of Trade and Industry. Reviews of existing research, rather than original research, may be of considerable value. In *Communities and crime reduction* (1988) international experts review research on various aspects of community crime prevention.

Reports are required by law on certain kinds of accidents: those involving civil aircraft and merchant ships, together with railway accidents. Each accident is investigated and a summary of its causes with recommendations is prepared by the Department of Transport's Air Accidents Investigation Branch, Marine Accident Investigation Branch or Railway Inspectorate. Major accidents may become the subject of a public enquiry, the results of which are published as a parliamentary publication. The *Investigation into the King's Cross Underground fire* (1989) was issued as a Command Paper (Cm.499).

Policy papers

Relatively few consultative 'green' papers appear as non- parliamentary publications. Examples include *Subscription television* (1987) and *Contracts for health services* (1990). Some Health and Safety Commission consultative documents on new regulations and codes of practice also appear as non-parliamentary publications. The great majority of definitive policy statements ('white papers') are parliamentary publications, but a small proportion are non-parliamentary, like *Modern languages in the school curriculum* (1988) or *Mergers policy* (1988).

Discussion papers from government departments set out to increase public awareness of a subject and to stimulate discussion rather than to lead to legislation directly. The *Curriculum matters* series from H.M. Inspectorate of Schools is designed to promote discussion and agreement about the aims and objectives of the curriculum. The series began in 1985 and by 1990 17 papers had appeared including *Mathematics from 5 to 16* (2nd ed., 1987) and *Information technology from 5 to 16* (1989).

Reviews and evaluations of the effects of existing policies allow the government to assess its successes and failures. The Consultancy Initiative programme is a key part of the Department of Trade and Industry's Enterprise Initiative: it was reviewed in *Evaluation of the Consultancy Initiatives* (1989). *Enforcing planning control* (1989) reviews the scope and effectiveness of the current enforcement mechanisms and suggests amendments. Case studies of good practice are a useful way of illustrating successful policy developments. The *Good practice in urban regeneration* series highlights good examples of policy initiation and operation on a range of topics including *Getting people into jobs* (1990) and *Developing sport and leisure* (1989). The outcome of policy reviews is not always favourable: the Equal Opportunities Commission's review of *Recent developments in childcare* (1989) studied the effects of several government initiatives and concluded that its policies have substantially hindered efforts to develop more and better quality childcare!

The final group of papers relating to policy concern the implementation of new policies being pursued by the government. They deal with how the policies will work and many discuss and illustrate methods and options. The working papers published in 1989—90 to follow the government white paper *Working for patients* (Cm.555) deal with different aspects of the reorganization of the National Health Service like *Self-governing hospitals* and *Practice budgets for General Medical Practitioners*. Compulsory competitive tendering for local authority services was introduced under the Local Government Act 1988. *Preparing for compulsory competition* (1989) discusses how local authorities should go about competitive tendering and the consequent restructuring needed. Specific guidance on implementing policies will be set out subsequently in circulars and letters.

Advice and guidance

Many of HMSO's publications are intended to disseminate information which the government feels should be widely known or to offer helpful advice and guidance. Government departments collect much information of value to a wider audience and can draw on the specialist expertise of staff and advisers. For some activities the government lays down guidelines and codes of practice to establish standards, improve safety and ensure satisfactory levels of performance.

Advisory publications

Many advisory leaflets are published directly by government departments and public bodies, but more substantial priced publications are issued by HMSO. The Ministry of Agriculture, Fisheries and Food (MAFF) has long been a major publisher of advisory material for farmers, horticulturists and the general public. Its extensive *Reference books* series covers topics from *Potato pests* (1989) to *Dairy herd fertility* (1984). Titles for the wider public include *Home preservation of fruit and vegetables*, a classic work first published in 1929 and now in its 14th edition (1989), and the colour-illustrated guide to identifying *Poisonous plants and fungi* (1988). Advice on safety matters is given by several bodies. *Essentials of health and safety at work* (2nd ed., 1989) is an inexpensive guide to preventing workplace accidents from the Health and Safety Executive. Advice on safety for teachers is provided by the Department of Education and Science in its *Safety series* which includes *Safety in outdoor education* (1989) dealing with the hazards of caving, skiing, canoeing and many other activities.

Training materials

Government departments have many training responsibilities: for their own staff, the armed forces, police, firemen and in some respects the general public. As a result HMSO publishes training handbooks, textbooks, self-instructional learning packs and videos. The standard textbook on fire-fighting is the Home Office's multi-volume *Manual of firemanship*, a new edition of which is being published. Of wider relevance are *Getting the best out of people* (1987) and *Understanding stress* (4 vols, 1987) which were developed as guides for Civil Service managers and trainers. Specialized training manuals for the armed forces contain much of value to civilians, as in the *Manual of seamanship* (rev. ed., 3 vols, 1979 – 83), the *Manual of map reading and land navigation* (2nd ed., 1989) and *Mountain rescue* (4th ed., 1980), the handbook for RAF mountain rescue teams. An unusual specialized manual is *Visitors welcome* (1988), a guide to excavators on the presentation and interpretation of information from archaeological excavations to help the general public make sense of sites.

Road users are a particular target of training handbooks and manuals because of the importance of safety. The Department of Transport is responsible for most of these including the widely used *Driving* (3rd ed., 1979), a manual covering all aspects of driving technique, and *Know your traffic signs* (3rd ed., 1989). *The highway code* (rev. ed., 1987) is the government's all-time bestseller and video editions in English (1988) and Bengali (1989) are now available, licensed by HMSO. *Keep on the safe side* (1989) is a new handbook for young cyclists on every aspect of safe cycling.

Codes of practice and guidelines

The highway code is one example of the considerable number of codes of practice and guidelines for various activities which have been drawn up by government departments. Some of these are legally enforceable while others are recommendations. A series of approved codes of practice have been developed on health and safety matters like *The control of asbestos at work* (1988) from the Health and Safety Commission and *The control of Legionellae in health care premises* (1988) from the Department of Health. The Home Office has issued four codes of practice on police powers, others on fire precautions and the *Code of practice for the housing and care of animals used in scientific procedures* (1989). Codes have also been introduced in other fields including food safety, industrial relations, local government and race relations. They aim to

57

establish standards which are accepted as the norm for the activity.

Guidelines exist for a wide range of topics of public concern from the safety of food to child abuse. In 1988 the Department of Health issued four publications offering guidance for nurses, health visitors, doctors, social workers and childcare agencies following the report on child abuse in Cleveland: *Child protection, Diagnosis of child sexual abuse, Working together* and *Protecting children*. Increased awareness of the dangers of food poisoning led to *Chilled and frozen. Guidelines on cook-chill and cook-freeze catering systems* (1989), also from the Department of Health. The introduction of the National Curriculum in schools has involved the setting of programmes of study and attainment targets for each subject. The first three titles were published in looseleaf format in 1989 covering mathematics, science and English. While aimed principally at teachers they are of considerable relevance to parents and school governors as well. The Health and Safety Executive issues nearly 200 *Guidance notes* through HMSO in five different series covering chemical safety, environmental hygiene, plant and machinery, medical matters and miscellaneous topics. Guidelines and recommended practice extend to many other areas of concern, like *Tackling racial violence and harassment in local authority housing* (1989) issued by the Department of the Environment for local authorities or *Instructions for consumer products* (1988) from the Department of Trade and Industry.

Reference sources

Much useful information from government bodies appears in the range of directories, yearbooks, almanacs, handbooks and other reference sources published by HMSO. These are designed to provide concise factual information quickly and simply. Many of the directories provide information on the civil service, the armed forces and diplomats. The annual *Civil Service yearbook* reveals the structure and organization of the civil service and the responsibilities of each department and section as well as naming senior staff. Each of the armed forces has a regular list of officers and establishments, with separately published lists of retired officers: *The Army list, The Navy list* and *The Air Force list*. Biographical details of British diplomats are included in the annual *Diplomatic service list* while foreign diplomats in London are recorded in *The London diplomatic list* (twice a year). Other directories include the *Directory of employers' associations, trade unions, joint organizations, etc.* (looseleaf, with frequent amendments), the two-volume *Census 1981 index of place names, England and Wales* (1985) listing places identified in the census with their location and population, and *Record repositories in Great Britain* (8th ed., 1987) which is a guide to record offices.

Two important yearbooks from HMSO give up-to-date information on countries. *Britain: an official handbook* (annual) provides a concise summary of British institutions and the country's economic, social, industrial and cultural framework, supported by statistics. *The Commonwealth yearbook* (annual) gives similar information more concisely for each Commonwealth country. Neither attempts to record and analyse current events which are covered in the monthly *Survey of current affairs*.

A number of annual almanacs published cooperatively by H.M. Nautical Almanac Office and the United States Naval Observatory contain basic data for navigation: *The astronomical almanac, The air almanac* and *The nautical almanac* are the main titles. Tables of weather data from the Meteorological Office appear in the *Monthly weather report* from HMSO, although it publishes most cumulated data itself.

HMSO publishes handbooks of essential information on a surprisingly wide range of topics both for the general public and for specialists. The complexities of the welfare benefits system are explained for claimants and their advisers in regularly updated looseleaf manuals: the *Income support manual* (1987–), the *Social fund manual* (1988–) and the *Housing benefits guidance manual* (2nd ed., 1988). *The industrial relations handbook* (new ed., 1980) outlines the structure of collective bargaining with descriptions of current arrangements in each industry for all concerned with industrial relations. The *Legal aid handbook* (8th ed., 1989) sets out entitlement to legal aid and the regulations affecting it for solicitors and advice workers. The *British regional geology* series of handbooks provides an explanatory text, maps, diagrams and photographs dealing with the geology of each region, e.g. *The Midland Valley of Scotland* (3rd ed., 1985). More specialized reference handbooks include the *Manual of nutrition* (9th ed., 1985) with details of the nutrient content of anything from fish fingers to yogurt and Coca Cola, and the *British Pharmacopoeia* (2 vols, new ed., 1988) which is used in many countries as the handbook for quality of medical preparations.

A major series of permanent reference value is the *British and Foreign State Papers* (170 vols, 1812–1978) which contains all the basic documents on British foreign policy for over 150 years. A new series of *Documents on British policy overseas* which collects key diplomatic papers since 1945 is currently being published with accompanying microfiches reproducing documents in full. HMSO issues many notable individual reference works. These include *People in Britain: a census atlas* (1980) with maps of population distribution, housing conditions and car ownership; *The complete plain words* (1986), an invaluable guide to clear English style; *Plain figures* (1986) which advises on the presentation of statistics; *Flags of all nations* (2nd ed., 1989) with colour illustrations of each flag; and *New religious movements* (1989), a guide to over 30 cults.

Periodicals

HMSO publishes three official newspapers: the *Belfast gazette* (weekly), the *Edinburgh gazette* (twice weekly) and the *London gazette* (daily). They hardly constitute entertaining reading but contain official notices and information. This includes Orders in (Privy) Council, public notices from local authorities on topics like parking restrictions or land acquisition for development, promotions in the armed forces, honours awarded, name changes by deed poll, and even the list of prize-winning premium bonds. They are particularly useful for notices relating to the winding-up and liquidation of companies and individual bankruptcies. A *Company law official notification supplement* (weekly on microfiche) lists details of newly registered companies. Twice a year supplements appear containing the Honours Lists which record who has been awarded life peerages, knighthoods or OBEs. A quarterly index to the *London gazette* is produced.

The majority of periodicals from HMSO are statistical or bibliographic and are mentioned in the appropriate section. Several periodicals formerly published by HMSO became non-HMSO official publications, were taken over by commercial publishers or were discontinued. Until 1987 *British business* was an HMSO publication; it was then published by the Department of Trade and Industry but was discontinued in September 1989. Surviving periodicals are mainly on health topics, notably *Health trends* and the *Prescribers' journal* (both quarterly). An exception is the *Meteorological magazine* (monthly) which contains scientific articles, reports of meetings, and news and reviews for weather scientists. A rare example of a new periodical from HMSO is *The pesticides register* (monthly) which began publication in 1989. It covers new developments for all those involved with pesticides, whether manufacturers, suppliers or users. These periodicals and a few other titles are available on subscription from HMSO.

Statistics and surveys

The government is in a unique position to collect and publish statistics on everything from the industrial production and export figures to the amount spent on drinks or gambling. The Rayner reviews of government statistical services in the early 1980s led to a cutback in publication of some series, but HMSO remains the major publisher of official statistics.[3] A significant amount of statistical data appears in parliamentary publications: answers to parliamentary questions in *Hansard*, regular statistical Command Papers, some reports of select committees and other investigative bodies, and annual reports (discussed in Chapter 2). Many of the major statistical publications are non-parliamentary, however, including the best known sources. Older statistics are usefully brought together in the microfiche collection of *British government publications containing statistics, 1801 – 1977* from Chadwyck-Healey, which is also available in subject sets.

The Rayner recommendations marked a significant change of attitude to the publication of official statistics. It is no longer sufficient for them to be of public interest or value. Rayner recommended that figures should be collected only because the government required them, and not primarily for publication. Statistical publications must cover their costs and commercial organizations should pay for current figures, like those in press releases. Many of his recommendations were accepted and as a result some titles ceased publication, the coverage of others was reduced, several data sets were published less frequently, and more titles became non-HMSO publications.[4] The effects have been felt much more among the social statistics than the economic ones, which may deprive people of the means of assessing the outcome of government policies.

The structure of the Government Statistical Service was altered in 1989 with the enlargement of the Central Statistical Office (CSO) and its changed status as a government department in its own right.[5] This followed a further review of *Government economic statistics* (HMSO, 1989) which paid more attention to quality and the requirements of users outside government. The CSO took over direct responsibility for one of the two major collecting agencies — the Business Statistics Office — and for all the Department of Trade and Industry's statistical series and for the Retail Price Index and the Family Expenditure Survey from the Department of Employment. It coordinates the rest of the Government Statistical Service which includes the statistics division of each government department and the other major collecting agency, the Office of Population Censuses and Surveys. Departments are each responsible for their own statistics, though the CSO tries to ensure that these figures are compiled consistently and to an agreed set of definitions. The CSO receives statistical data from departments and produces the main summary statistics.

The *Guide to official statistics* (6th ed., 1990) is the main directory for HMSO and other official statistics. It is updated every four years or so, but the latest developments can be found in the quarterly periodical *Statistical news*. A short free guide *Government statistics: a brief guide to sources* is available from the CSO and is updated quite frequently. This guide can also be found in *Key data*.

Summary statistics

The government statistics with which people are most familiar are the range of general summary statistics prepared by the CSO. *Key data* is a reasonably priced annual compilation intended mainly for students which presents selected figures on a wide range of social and economic topics from incomes and prices to hospital waiting lists and organ transplants. The *Annual abstract of statistics* contains many series over a ten-year period for every aspect of economic, social and industrial life from population or national income and expenditure to cinema attendances. The *Monthly digest of statistics* presents a more limited range of tables for figures updated monthly or quarterly. A series of 'Trends' publications present the figures in a less daunting manner with charts and diagrams and articles to comment on them. *Economic trends* (monthly) brings together all the main economic indicators for the UK economy and its *Annual supplement* provides long runs of the key statistics going back up to 40 years. *Social trends* (annual) is the most popular and interesting of these publications; it gives a concise summary of the main social data: employment, leisure, personal income and expenditure, health, education, etc. *Regional trends* analyses the major statistics from eating habits to health and employment on a regional basis for all UK regions. Separate annual statistical digests are published for Scotland, Wales and Northern Ireland, but these are now published directly and not by HMSO. These general digests of statistics are prepared from more detailed figures, many of which are also published by HMSO.

Major collecting agencies

The two agencies most closely involved in the collection of statistics are the Office of Population Censuses and Surveys (OPCS) and the Business Statistics Office (BSO). The OPCS collects census figures, registrations of births, deaths and marriages, and medical and mortality statistics for England and Wales.[6] The Registrars General for Scotland and Northern Ireland collect the equivalent figures for their countries. Censuses have been held since 1801, usually at ten-year intervals. The published reports which appear in many volumes with detailed reports for each county and analyses of workplace, household composition, migration, etc form a unique demographic and social record. The annual *Key population and vital statistics* and *Population projections* for up to 40 years are particularly useful to planners. The OPCS is responsible for continuing and special surveys on behalf of other government departments, though this part of its work has been cut back. It prepares a number of regular surveys. The annual *Family expenditure survey* shows expenditure on goods and services at different income levels. The *General household survey* covers population, housing, employment, education and health matters, highlighting different topics each year. The *Labour force survey* deals with the characteristics of the workforce and is an important source of ethnic data. Special surveys include six reports in the *OPCS surveys of disability in Great Britain* series (1988–89) and *Smoking among secondary school children in England in 1988* (SS 1291, 1989).

The Business Statistics Office is responsible for collecting most figures from manufacturers, retailers and service industries. Its main publications are the *Business monitors*, which are issued in three series: Production, Service and distributive, and Miscellaneous. They give figures for sales, output, stocks, wages, etc for products and services from fertilizers and motor vehicles to retail sales or ice cream production. Until 1989 169 monitors were published quarterly in the production series. Following a review of the collection of business statistics, the majority moved to annual publication with just 41 monitors continuing on a quarterly basis. This change also affects the *Annual census of production* reports for each industry in the *Production monitors* series. The first of the new annual business monitors covering 1989 figures was published in mid-1990. These short-term and annual figures are useful to managers assessing the performance of their company and the state of their industry as well as to economists. A free leaflet *Business monitors* lists the titles currently published.

Specialized statistics

HMSO publishes a range of statistical compilations relating to the economy, housing, agriculture, trade, transport, taxation, education, justice and the environment. These usually appear annually presenting a range of tables on the topic, but some are issued more frequently like the monthly *Financial statistics* which records the money supply, public sector borrowing, and exchange and interest rates. Other essential sources on the economy are the *UK national accounts* and *UK balance of payments* (both annual).

Since the Rayner reviews of statistical services HMSO tends to publish the major figures for each topic but more frequent or more detailed figures may be published directly by the relevant department. Statistics specifically for Scotland, Wales and Northern Ireland are mostly published separately by the Scottish Office, the Welsh Office and the appropriate Northern Ireland department. The *Transport statistics Great Britain* are published annually by HMSO but the quarterly *Transport statistics* are issued by the Department of Transport. The *Statistics of education*, an annual six-volume set, is no longer published by HMSO but is available from the Department of Education and Science. HMSO produces only the *Education statistics for the UK* (annual) in one volume. The main criminal and judicial statistics appear as parliamentary publications.

Current figures and the CSO Databank

The most recent statistics on a topic will usually first be issued as a press notice by the CSO or the relevant department and may be mentioned by national newspapers. Such press releases are issued according to a timetable which is announced in advance. Some figures will not be republished elsewhere and these are particularly hard to trace. Some government departments have their own periodical to record recent figures. These may be published by HMSO, like the *Employment gazette* (monthly) with figures for manpower, earnings, hours worked, unemployment and strikes, as well as the retail price index. Others are issued by the department directly, mostly as priced publications such as *Energy trends* (monthly) and the *OPCS monitors* (varying frequencies). Until 1989 *British business* from the DTI was a major source of current statistics. It has been partly replaced by a series of *Business bulletins* published directly by the CSO and available on subscription.

Much CSO statistical data is available in electronic form as the CSO databank, including the *Economic trends* dataset, national accounts, balance of payments, price indexes, and employment and earnings figures. The CSO databank is available on tape or disc and online through Datastream, DRI and WEFA but not directly from the CSO. These hosts are not used by many libraries, but it is also available from the ESRC

Data Archive via the Joint Academic Network (JANET). There is considerable scope for more widespread exploitation of government statistical data in online form.

Quality of statistics

Much concern has been expressed about several aspects of government statistics in the past few years. This includes the discontinuation of some sets of figures and the reduction in publication frequency of others. This can greatly diminish the value of the figures, such as those for income distribution which now appear only once every four years. Revision of definitions has changed the nature of several sets of figures, most notoriously those for unemployment where the definition of 'unemployed' was adjusted 24 times between 1979 and 1989. Speed of publication is another problem: most statistics are not available as quickly as users expect them to be. Titles may be misleading in this respect: the *Social security statistics 1990* actually covers 1988/89 data. Users must also look closely at what geographical area of the UK the statistics cover: England only, England and Wales, Great Britain (England, Scotland, Wales) or the United Kingdom of Great Britain and Northern Ireland. Truly national statistics can be hard to find for some subjects as the government departments collect only for the area they administer. Collection frequency for figures on the same topic may differ in the constituent parts of the UK: employment figures are monthly in England, Scotland and Wales but quarterly in Northern Ireland. Commercial publishers of statistics can add value to official figures by providing convenient aggregations of data. Statistics have also been affected by such errors as the under-estimating of the retail price index and the over-estimating of consumer spending in 1987-88 by the Department of Employment.

A review of arrangements for the production of key statistics, *Government economic statistics. A scrutiny report*, was completed in 1989 and the enlarged CSO is committed to improving the quality of statistics. It began a full review of CSO statistical publications in late 1989. Meanwhile users of statistics should treat them with caution, remembering Disraeli's assertion that 'There are three kinds of lies: lies, damned lies and statistics'.

Historical, archaeological and cultural publications

HMSO is a significant publisher in the historical and archaeological fields with a surprising range of popular and scholarly publications. These arise from the work of individual government departments, museums and bodies like the Public Record Office (which is the main repository of government records) or the Royal Commission on Historical Monuments, which publishes inventories of archaeological sites and historic buildings. HMSO usually marks significant anniversaries with publications: the 50th anniversary of the outbreak of World War II produced a spate of publications including facsimiles of *The Battle of Britain* (1989) which was first published in 1941 and sold over two million copies by the end of the war, and of a German account of *The U-Boat war in the Atlantic 1939–1945* (1989).

History

Popular histories with potential for large sales form part of HMSO's output. *Parliament and the Glorious Revolution 1688–1988* was HMSO's colour souvenir booklet to mark the tercentenary of the overthrow of James II. *Big Ben and the clock tower* (1987) tells the story of this famous clock and features a fold-out illustration of the tower. Scottish official bodies have produced a number of interesting popular illustrated histories, all published by HMSO, including *Bonnie Prince Charlie* (1988), *The First World War* (1987) and *The enterprising Scot* (1988). *Tracing your ancestors in the Public Record Office* (4th ed., 1990) and *Tracing your Scottish ancestors* (1990) are practical guides for the many people wanting to find out about their predecessors. The Geological Museum's lavishly illustrated booklets on geological topics, including *Volcanoes* (1974) and *Moon, Mars and meteorites* (1984), proved popular. Several titles on apects of Britain's railways come from the National Railway Museum and the Science Museum, of which *Palaces on wheels: royal carriages at the National Railway Museum* (1981) is one of the most interesting.

HMSO is a publisher of more scholarly histories, though some of these become popular sellers because of their subject. The Historical Section of the Cabinet Office has been responsible for the publication of official histories of the First and Second World Wars and the more recent peacetime histories series. These are major multi-volume series covering every conceivable aspect of the two wars, not just the military campaigns. The volumes which have perhaps attracted the most attention have been those on *British intelligence in the Second World War* (5 vols, 1979–90), publication of the later volumes of which was delayed because of sensitivity over security matters. The first volume of a new *Peacetime series* on *The health services since the war* appeared in 1988. Several histories of government departments or of aspects of their work have been published, including *Shoes and ships and sealing-wax* (1986), a history of the Board of Trade, and *Loaves and fishes* (1989), an illustrated history of the Ministry of Agriculture, Fisheries and Food from 1889 to the present.

As well as issuing historical works, HMSO also publishes guides to historical sources to help researchers. The Royal Commission on Historical Manuscripts produces a *Guide to sources of British history* series describing the papers of cabinet ministers, diplomats, scientists and churchmen. The Public Record Office issues a useful series of handbooks including *Making sense of the census* (1989) and *Naval records for genealogists* (1988).

Archaeology

The government is deeply involved in archaeology, especially through the Royal Commissions on historical monuments which publish detailed inventories of the archaeological sites and historic buildings of each county and outstanding towns. These are expensive but thorough and illustrated with maps, aerial photographs and drawings of each site, e.g. *An inventory of the ancient monuments in Brecknock, Part 2: Hill-forts and Roman remains* (1987) from the Royal Commission on Ancient and Historical Monuments in Wales. The exhaustive five-volume inventory of historic buildings in York was completed in 1981, with a photographic record of each building. Some publications deal with individual sites or particular kinds of monument, e.g. *The archaeology of Bokerley Dyke* (1990) and *Churches of south-east Wiltshire* (1987). English Heritage archaeological reports on excavations and sites were obtainable only from them, but since late 1988 titles can also be ordered from HMSO. Several publications present well-illustrated studies of everyday buildings of the past from *Workers' housing in West Yorkshire 1750–1820* (1986) to *Scottish castles and fortifications* (1986). The photographs in *Hotels and restaurants* (1981) and *London's bridges* (1983) are drawn from the National Monuments Record Photographic Archives, which was started in 1941 to build up a systematic record of English architecture.

Guidebooks

Guidebooks are a declining category of HMSO publications as several major series are now issued by other publishers. The effect in some cases is to make them more difficult to obtain. The guides to ancient monuments, now published by the public bodies set up to run them in

England and Wales (English Heritage and Cadw), are a good example of this. The staid National Park guides from HMSO have been replaced by an attractively packaged series from Webb & Bower/Michael Joseph. The Countryside Commission's *Long distance footpath guides*, which were published by HMSO, have mostly been superseded by the *National Trail guides* published jointly by the Countryside Commission, the Ordnance Survey and Aurum Press. Walking guides for Scotland and Northern Ireland are still published by HMSO, like *The West Highland Way* (1990) and *Mourne mountain walks* (1990). Very few guidebooks have been taken over from other publishers by HMSO, but one example is the 1990 reprint of *Hampton Court Palace*, originally published by Kaye & Ward.

Other guidebooks still issued by HMSO include Forestry Commission guides like *Explore the New Forest* (2nd ed., 1987) and those for Scottish historic buildings and monuments, which are the responsibility of the Scottish Development Department. The *Exploring Scotland's heritage* series (1984–87) comprises eight attractive illustrated guides to interesting and well-preserved monuments in each Scottish region. Guides to individual Scottish sites are also produced, like the inexpensive and attractive booklet on *Iona* (1983). A perennially popular guide is *The Houses of Parliament: an illustrated guide to the Palace of Westminster* now in its 14th edition, 1988. In view of the demand for many of its past guidebooks HMSO has lost some potentially profitable publications.

Cultural publications

HMSO formerly published a substantial number of museum and gallery publications and some of these are still available until they go out of print. Examples include the 20 titles in the *V & A introductions to the decorative arts series* ranging from *English stained glass* (1986) to *Netsuke* (1982). *Sectional list no. 73. Museums and galleries* (1990) conveniently brings together these titles and some new ones. The national museums and galleries are now independent agencies (discussed in the next chapter) and relatively few new items are issued by HMSO. The only HMSO title from the Victoria and Albert Museum in 1988 was *Playing cards in the V & A*, while in 1990 it published *The photographic work of Calvert Richard Jones* for the Science Museum. The Public Record Office has produced collections of advertising posters in *Cocoa and corsets* (1984) and *Buy and build* (1986). The National Portrait Gallery has issued a number of catalogues through HMSO including a new edition of its popular *Royal faces* (1990). A series of 11 illustrated regional guides to *Exploring museums* for the Museums and Galleries Commission appeared between 1989 and 1991. Occasional publications from other government bodies relate to the arts, like *Tapestries and textiles at the Palace of Holyroodhouse* (1988) from the Lord Chamberlain's Office.

Bibliographic and research sources
Apart from its own catalogues and lists, HMSO publishes a number of bibliographies, current awareness services and research listings. These include the *Kew record of taxonomic literature* (annual) which is a current subject bibliography of books, articles and reports relating to vascular plants, and *Contents of recent economics journals*, a weekly current awareness service compiled by the Department of Trade and Industry Library and Information Centre. *Social service abstracts* is an important monthly abstracting service which records the recent literature and is available online as part of the DHSS-DATA database on DATASTAR. The Department of Health's *DH yearbook of research and development* is published annually by HMSO and incorporates research supported by the Department of Social Security. The annual *Report on forest research* provides an overview of research carried out for and by the Forestry Commission. HMSO took over publication of George Ottley's massive *A Bibliography of British railway history* (1983) and produced a *Supplement* (1988) recording a further 5,000 books and pamphlets. Most other bibliographical publications and research listings are issued directly by government department libraries.

GOVERNMENT DEPARTMENTS AS PUBLISHERS
HMSO's output on behalf of government departments is considerable but it is outweighed by the amount of material published directly by departments. The Welsh Office sponsored just under 350 HMSO titles in 1986, almost all of them joint publications with other government departments, but its directly published titles amounted to over 500. In 1989 the DTI's recorded output was nearly 600 titles compared with just 34 HMSO non-parliamentary publications (excluding Business Statistics Office publications, which were transferred to the Central Statistical Office in late 1989). An equally striking comparison is the 1987 total of almost 1000 titles listed in the *Catalogue of British official publications* (CoBOP) from the DHSS and related organizations as against just over 100 HMSO non-parliamentary publications. CoBOP listed over 6,000 non-HMSO publications from government departments and their

associated bodies in 1988. This is not necessarily a complete record. Some titles, particularly those from regional offices, remain unknown as they may not even be notified to the compilers of departmental publications lists let alone sent to the British Library under the legal deposit regulations. Differing ideas of what constitutes a 'publication' further complicate the issue, leading to titles going unrecorded.

The trend away from publishing through HMSO became marked in the 1960s and 1970s when government departments first began to collect and list their publications systematically. The number of titles published directly is still growing: the recorded output of non-HMSO titles from the then Departments of Industry and Trade and the DHSS in 1980 was 157 and 528 respectively, compared with 598 in 1989 from the DTI and 976 in 1987 from the then DHSS. Public awareness of the existence of these publications was increased by the debates on official secrecy and the continuing campaign for greater openness in government. The 'Croham directive' of 1977 on the disclosure of official information encouraged government departments to publish more of the information produced as background to policy decisions.[7] Despite these moves, most non-HMSO publications of government departments remain much less well known than their HMSO counterparts because few receive the same amount of publicity or are as easily available as HMSO titles.

There is now a greater likelihood that departmental publications will be priced: the *OPCS monitors* were free departmental publications until 1987 when subscriptions were introduced. Some departments are reluctant to charge because of the administrative costs involved, especially for relatively small amounts. The use of computers for processing of orders, mailing lists and accounts has made it easier to charge, however, and a few departments have a centralized unit. Publications from the Scottish departments are available through the Scottish Office Library Publications Sales Unit, for instance.

A considerable amount of free material is still being issued, mainly small-scale publications like leaflets, short pamphlets, newsletters and notices. More substantial publications which are still free include the DTI's informative guide to *The single market: the facts* (5th ed., 1990); and the report on *Performance indicators for the probation service* (1988) from the Home Office. HMSO has taken over the publishing of some former departmental titles which it considered to be commercially viable. The 1989−90 edition of *Door to door*, a guide to transport for disabled people, was the first to be published by HMSO; several previous editions had been published directly by the Department of Transport. Departmental material may also be issued by non-official publishers: *Paying for training*, issued by the Department of Education and Science in 1986, was an unexpected success. Demand led to two reprints and new editions in 1988 and 1990, the latter published by the Planning Exchange. The range of non-HMSO departmental publications is fairly similar to the output of HMSO already discussed. This is a source of confusion as many people expect publications which are issued by departments all to be from HMSO. ISBNs are helpful in distinguishing HMSO from non-HMSO: 010 and 011 prefixes (and 0337 for HMSO Northern Ireland) are always HMSO publications; departments have their own ISBNs for directly published material. The absence of an ISBN also suggests a non-HMSO publication. Examples of most of the same kinds of publications can be found in departmentally published material, but with fewer historical and cultural, legislative and training publications and more in the advisory, research, periodicals and bibliographic sources groups.[8] The major difference between HMSO and departmental publications lies in the sheer volume of mostly brief information and advisory publications, newsletters and press releases issued free of charge by departments.

Free departmental publications

Free publications are completely outside of HMSO's scope, yet form the bulk of the output of government departments. Free information and advisory publications are produced for a variety of reasons ranging from the need to communicate with local authorities, companies or health service employees to giving advice on energy saving, health or shopping to the general public. This material may have a very big potential audience and be used by people who consult no other official publications. Some of it is widely available in the community through post offices, job centres, social security offices, libraries and advice agencies. Other titles are publicized through adverts in the press and on radio and television. The effectiveness of this publicity is demonstrated by the demand for the Home Office's guide to *Practical ways to crack crime* (1988), over three million copies of which had been distributed by late 1989.

Information publications

The government issues a large number of publications to provide people with information about their rights and duties and about practical problems of living, working, having children, buying goods and services and so on.[9] Probably the most familiar are the former DHSS leaflets on welfare benefits. These were divided into two separate series from

71

different sources in 1988. The Department of Health publishes those relating to the Health Service like *D11 NHS dental treatment* and *G11 NHS sight tests and vouchers for glasses*. The Department of Social Security publishes the larger series (over 40 titles in 1989) ranging from the *Young people's guide to social security* and *Sickness benefit* to *Help when someone dies*. The Office of Fair Trading and DTI's leaflets and booklets on consumer protection matters like *Your place in the sun, or is it?* (a guide for time-share buyers from the DTI) and *Don't wave your money goodbye* (OFT) are also widely distributed through libraries and advice centres. Some information publications deal with practical problems like *Bothered by noise? What you can do about it* (1989) from the Department of the Environment. The introduction of new developments often leads to information publications like *The student top-up loans scheme: an outline* (1990) from the Department of Education and Science.

Some departments offer general factual information in summary form in their free publications. The Central Office of Information distributes a wide range of information about Britain, but most is available only outside the UK (except on microfiche from Chadwyck-Healey). The Scottish Information Office has a series of regularly updated fact sheets on different aspects of life in Scotland covering topics like the fishing industry, North Sea oil and gas and the Scottish economy. Factual information from other departments includes the Department of Energy's *Taking power from water: water technology in Britain* (1989) which explains recent developments and *An outline of United Kingdom competition policy* (1990) from the Office of Fair Trading which explains this complex subject. Information packs are produced for schools, including the *Project fire* pack from the Home Office and the Department of Energy's *Practical energy projects* pack with workcards, computer programmes and a teacher's guide.

Explanations of legislation

A distinct group of advisory leaflets set out to explain legislation and show how it affects the individual. This is a vital aspect of publishing since legislation is often difficult for the lay person to understand, yet everyone is assumed to know the law. The community charge which replaced the rating system in 1990 is explained in simple terms in *You and the community charge* (Department of the Environment, 1989). A series of more detailed booklets on different aspects of the scheme, like *Students and the community charge*, is available. The Department of

Employment has leaflets providing guidance to current employment legislation. Measures like the Employment Act 1988 require explanatory material such as *Trade union executive elections* (PL 866) and *Industrial action and the law* (PL 869 and 870). These are available from employment offices and job centres. Similar guides to legislation are put out by other departments and public bodies including the Equal Opportunities Commission and the Legal Aid Board. There is a strong case for extending the provision of such guides to cover much more legislation, though HMSO has published more titles of this nature recently.

Promotional material

Free publications are used to increase awareness of the work and services of government departments. *Her Majesty's Treasury* (1988) is a quite lavish guide to the organization and work of the Treasury for the general public. *British aid* is a colour illustrated booklet showing how the Overseas Development Administration manages the aid programme and what the money is spent on. *DTI − a guide for business* is an extremely useful regularly revised booklet listing contacts and responsibilities of the Department to help business people find the right person to talk to. *Your guide to our employment, training and enterprise programmes* from the Department of Employment is a handy summary of the schemes available and who to contact. Publications are also used to show the implications of government policies, like the *Working for patients* and *You and your GP* leaflets on the reform of the Health Service. Similarly, the introduction of the National Curriculum in state schools is briefly explained in *National Curriculum. A guide for parents* (1989) which shows how it will affect what children are taught.

Promotional material also supports government campaigns on health, safety, crime, driving, energy saving and many other matters. The Home Office's crime prevention campaign offered a free handbook on *Practical ways to crack crime* (2nd ed., 1988) to underpin its press and television advertising. The Department of Energy's Energy Efficiency Office has been running energy saving campaigns for several years. It issues *Handy hints to save energy in your home* (1989) to alert home owners to potential savings and provides practical guidance in *Your home energy survey* pack with booklets on insulation methods. Somewhat confusingly, the Department of the Environment also offers advice about energy saving in homes.

Advisory publications

Each government department has a range of expertise which is valuable to the general public or to particular groups. Several departments produce a range of advisory publications to help on anything from slurry handling to choosing retirement homes for elderly people. The Department of the Environment's series of advice booklets on housing matters includes *House renovation grants* (1990) and *'He wants me out': protection against harassment and illegal eviction* (1989). The Department of Health issues *The traveller's guide to health*, with changes noted on Prestel, as well as a guide to reducing *Medical costs abroad*. It has also participated in a joint venture with the voluntary organizations Age Concern and Help the Aged in giving advice on how to *Keep warm, keep well* which is produced in 11 different languages.

The Ministry of Agriculture, Fisheries and Food (MAFF) publishes free leaflets for farmers and horticulturalists on anything from *Preparing for storage of apples* (1987) to *Small scale poultry keeping* (1987). Many are ADAS (Agricultural Development and Advisory Service) booklets and pamphlets which are now available only through local ADAS advisers, but a substantial number of free pamphlets are still available from MAFF. It also produces advice on food handling including a guide to *Food safety* (1989) and *Food additives: the balanced approach* (1987) as a result of greater consumer concern about the food we eat.

The Department of Employment's Small Firms Service offers some free material to those thinking of starting a business, notably the booklets on *Starting and running your own business*, *How to start exporting*, and *Accounting for a small firm*. It acts as an advisory service and provides initial counselling free. The Inland Revenue also gives advice for those *Starting in business* (IR 28) as well as to other tax payers in its extensive series of regularly revised booklets on income and capital taxes and their effects on different groups, like *Income tax and pensioners* (IR 4). The Department of Education and Science suggests how parents can help support their children's education in a handbook on *Our changing schools* (1989). Some of the Home Office advisory material is intended for a much more limited audience, especially *Life sentence: your questions answered* (1986). These examples are only a very small sample of the range of advisory material available from government departments.

Newsletters and periodicals

Most government departments produce free newsletters and periodicals to ensure regular communication of news, views and policies. A few are for a general audience like *VFM*, a colour magazine for 11 to 16-year-olds from the Office of Fair Trading, but most are intended for a specialist readership interested in matters which concern the department. The Department of Trade and Industry has over a dozen periodicals and newsletters for small businesses, exporters, manufacturers, and those concerned with innovation. Titles include *Manufacturing intelligence newsletter* (two a year), the *Channel tunnel fixed link newsletter* (monthly) and *In business now* (six a year). The Home Office's periodicals range from brief newsletters to substantial journals with lengthy articles by specialists. They include *Crime prevention news* (quarterly), *New life: the prison service chaplaincy review* (annual) and *Civil protection* (quarterly). Most of these periodicals are free to people who qualify for inclusion on the mailing list, though some titles like the *Health bulletin* (Scottish Home and Health Department, bi-monthly) are available on subscription.

Careers literature

This is produced by a number of government departments to attract suitable recruits. The Civil Service Commission is responsible for general recruitment to middle and high level posts in government departments and issues careers literature directly for a range of professions e.g. architects, economists, scientists. Some departments issue their own recruitment literature for specialist posts like the Home Office's range on careers in the prison service (*The inside story: your career as a prison officer* is one of the titles!). Recruitment of junior staff is the responsibility of individual departments and is encouraged by leaflets like *Join the civil service through YTS* (1988) from the DTI.

Press releases

Every government department issues news releases to inform newspapers, television and radio on a wide range of topics. These include ministerial speeches and policy announcements, new legislation, the latest statistics, appointments to public bodies, government proposals for consultation, comment on current campaigns, reports of committees and investigations, and even *Clocks go back — reminder*. Hundreds are produced each year: the Home Office list of 'selected' news releases included over 360 in 1989. Some are far more lengthy than their name suggests: 20 of the 91 Department of Education and Science press notices listed in CoBOP in 1989 had six or more pages and two reached 25 pages. They should be totally ephemeral, but some are used as a substitute for publication of the information in any other form. The fastest and most accessible source for press releases is the Hermes database available from FT Profile. It provides the full text of press releases issued by most government departments and some other bodies like the Equal Opportunities Commission and the Health and Safety Executive. Only selected press notices from the Scottish Office and the Welsh Office are included and there is just a bibliographic reference for some statistical material. The latest press releases (issued on the previous working day) are in a separate file, Hermes Daily. Departmental lists of publications usually only include a selection of news releases (Home Office) or may omit them altogether (DTI). A few departments, like the Department of Health, include press releases in their own database or issue a printed list like *DES press notices and statistical bulletins* (annual).

Circulars, memoranda and guidance

Official communications from government departments to local authorities, health authorities, industry and other groups take the form of circulars, memoranda, guidance notes, letters and notices. Most of them are short but they may contain important information on government policy, new legislation, safety matters or changes in administrative practice. As with news releases some departments issue hundreds every year. The Welsh Office issued over 150 circulars in 1986 on many topics including agriculture, education, housing, health, planning and transport. Home Office circulars include those on *Alcohol and disorder* (No. 74, 1988) and *Anglicisation of Irish names* (No. 24/4, 1988). It also issued *Home Office guidance on the use of neuromuscular blocking agents* (1988) and *Supervision and after-care of conditionally discharged restricted patients* (1987), three sets of guidance notes for social supervisors, multidisciplinary clinical teams and supervising psychiatrists. The Department of Health has several series, including *Advance letters* to health authorities on staff pay and conditions of service and *Health notices* to doctors and hospitals. It issues *Health circulars, notices and other guidance material: index* to keep track of them all. Guidelines and codes of practice may also be non-HMSO publications. The Scottish Home and Health Department has issued a code of practice on *Confidentiality of personal health information* (1990), for instance.

Export information

The range of departmental publications of value to a particular group can be seen in the Department of Trade and Industry's Export Initiative.

The DTI offers a large amount of information and advice about exporting and export markets in printed and electronic forms. Much of this information is restricted to exporters and potential exporters, but some is generally available. Within DTI there are four overseas trade divisions, each with export market branches dealing with groups of countries, like the Middle East branch. *The Export Initiative guide to exporting* (1989) explains how DTI and other official agencies can help at each stage of the export process. The well-known *Hints to exporters* series from the British Overseas Trade Board offers up-to-date information about individual countries in regularly revised booklets (59 published in 1989). They cover the country's economy, social customs, regulations, and methods of doing business. *Country profiles* each concentrate on marketing information for one country, but fewer are published each year (30 in 1989). Market reports relating to specific products in individual countries pinpoint opportunities for exporters, e.g. *USA: menswear: a market analysis* (1989) and *The Netherlands: equipment for the disabled* (1989). Current information on trade opportunities is also available as a current awareness service from the Export Intelligence Service which is provided online by FT Profile. The DTI maintains an in-house database of export information, BOTIS, which is available to users of the Export Market Information Centre.

Special emphasis has been given to the 1992 Single European Market campaign with substantial and informative printed guides like *The single market: the facts* (5th ed., 1990), which went through five editions in the 18 months after publication, and the Spearhead online database of single market information available from FT Profile.[10] *Single market news* (1988-) is issued quarterly to provide current information and case studies. A series of action guides like *1992 − for you: an action guide for smaller firms* (1989) and *Keeping your product on the market* (1990) deal with different aspects of the single market which affect businesses and the professions. Posters and videos help to spread the message more widely. *Overseas trade* (ten a year) is a more general periodical featuring export news and market opportunities. At present most of the printed information on the Single Market is free whereas information from the online databases must be paid for.

The enormous quantity of free advisory and information material is clear from the range discussed here. However, these are not the only free publications to be issued by departments and many of the titles referred to in the next section are also free.

Types of departmental publications

Apart from the types of free publications already described, departments also publish most of the kinds of material discussed in the section on HMSO's non-parliamentary publications. In addition, audiovisual materials and posters are produced by departments but rarely by HMSO.

Administrative and enquiry reports

The majority of administrative reports are published by HMSO or issued direct by public bodies. A small number are published departmentally including the annual reports of the Property Services Agency and the British Overseas Trade Board. Enquiry and advisory reports, however, are more common. Two substantial series are the result of the work of inspectors who are required to make evaluations and report back to the minister. Several hundred reports of Her Majesty's Inspectorate (HMI) on inspections of individual schools and colleges in England, Scotland and Wales are published each year. Broader issues arising from these reports may be taken up, as in *Schools in Hackney: some issues* (1990) which identified areas of concern following the transfer of responsibilities for education from the Inner London Education Authority to Hackney. The reports to the Home Office of HM Chief Inspector of Prisons on conditions in prisons, detention centres and youth custody centres are very detailed. *The Report on HM Prison Pentonville* (1988), for instance, is 171 pages long and includes a statement by the Home Secretary.

The committees and working parties reporting to government departments may have their reports issued departmentally. This does not necessarily mean that they are less important than those published by HMSO. The *Report of the working group on the prevention of violence associated with licensed premises* (Home Office, 1986) dealt with a matter of concern to many people, while the report on *A strategy for the reduction of bridge bashing* (1988) published by HMSO was of more interest to the Department of Transport than to the wider public. Many valuable reports are issued directly by departments. Department of Health reports include the *Report of the working party on the supply of donor organs for transplantation* (1987) and *Nurse prescribing* (1990), which recommends that nurses with certain qualifications should be allowed to prescribe medicines. The Home Office has studied subjects like fouling of public places by dogs and the report on the pilot project to test the effectiveness of a new *Removal of canine faeces byelaw* (1987) assesses experience of implementing it in four local authority districts. The report is accompanied by *Model byelaws for the regulation of dogs* (the 'poop scoop' byelaws) and Home Office Circular no. 21/1987 to local authorities advising them of the byelaws they can make and suggesting how to encourage people (and dogs?) to comply with them.

Some advisory reports are commissioned from professional consultants rather than being produced by committees. The Scottish Office employed Research Scotland Ltd to assess the *Future of public sector housing in the Scottish new towns* (1989), for instance. Occasionally an interim report may be published departmentally while the final report appears from HMSO. This happened with the *Piper Alpha technical investigation*, the interim report of which was published by the Department of Energy in 1988, while the report of *The public enquiry into the Piper Alpha disaster* appeared as a Command Paper in 1990 (Cm.1310). By no means all reports of enquiries are published: the energy efficiency report on the Palace of Westminster, commissioned by the Property Services Agency, was not published when it was completed in late 1989 and the government refused to spend money on the energy-saving measures recommended.

Technical and research reports
Technical and research reports are more likely to be departmental than HMSO publications because of the limited potential readership and therefore sales for most. They are suitable for cheaper copying methods and lower standards of production. Some government departments, like Education and Science, publish the majority of their research through HMSO. In other cases the main report series may be published by HMSO but more specialized papers appear departmentally: the Home Office *Research studies* series is HMSO but its *Research and Planning Unit papers* and those of its Scientific Research and Development Branch (SRDB) are departmental publications. Titles include *The role and function of police community liaison officers* (Research and Planning Unit paper no. 51, 1988) and the *Advanced criminal intelligence analysis evaluation report* (SRDB 32/89, 1989). Similarly, the Department of Energy's *Offshore technology reports* series is published by HMSO but it issues both a series of full reports (18 in 1989) and a large number of short *Project profiles* (over 70 in 1989) directly. Most of the Department of Employment's research, like *Ethnic minorities and employment practice: a study of six organizations* (no.76, 1990), is published by the Department in its *Research papers series* rather than by HMSO.

Some projects involve cooperation between government departments, trade associations and other bodies like individual companies. *Plastics recycling in Europe* (1989) is a cooperative project involving the DTI, the British Plastics Foundation and the British Soft Drinks Association. A number of reviews of research drawing on previous studies are published departmentally, like *Volunteering and unemployment: a literature review* (1990) from the Scottish Office Central Research Unit.

Policy papers

Although definitive policy statements (white papers) are almost all published by HMSO, the position is reversed with consultative documents. In the 1989-90 parliamentary session all but seven of the 240 consultative documents listed in the *Weekly information bulletin* were non-HMSO publications. Considerable problems may be caused by their appearing in this way: although they are listed quite quickly, it can be difficult for the public to get hold of them before the time limit for discussion has passed. Certainly this was the case with the Department of Education and Science's important consultative papers on the National Curriculum which were published in late November 1988 with comments invited before the end of January 1989. Many consultative papers of major significance are published departmentally: the DES proposals on the National Curriculum like *English for ages 5 to 11* affect the education of all pupils in state schools. The Department of Transport's consultative paper on *Seat belt wearing* (1990) outlines the case for compulsory wearing of rear seat belts by all passengers. The DTI is also an important producer of consultative documents: 15 appeared in 1989 on such topics as insider dealing, annual returns of companies, and portable phones. Some departments make available the responses to their consultative papers: the Scottish Office made available public responses to over 50 papers in 1989. Government responses to the comments received in consultation exercises may also be published departmentally: *Private finance for roads − government response to consultation on 'New roads by new means'* (1990) was published by the Department of Transport. A cumulative subject index of consultative papers and discussion documents appears in the *Sessional information digest*.

Reviews of government policies are often prepared by departments to assess their effectiveness and to look at possible ways of improving them. *Support for design: final evaluation report* (1988) is one of a small series of *Assessment papers* looking at aspects of DTI policy, while the *Review of DTI statistics* (1989) presaged the removal of many statistical publications from the department. The Home Office has carried out *A scrutiny of grants under Section 11 of the Local Government Act 1986* (1989) which support a range of projects with ethnic minority groups. Reviews can be used to communicate what has been achieved and to set out the continuing strategy as in *Criminal justice* (1986) and *Tackling crime* (1989), both from the Home Office, or *Progress on cities* (1989) from the Department of the Environment's Inner Cities Division.

Occasional discussion papers appear as non-HMSO publications: the DES's *Crime prevention in schools: building-related aspects. A discussion paper* (1986) provides an account of current crime prevention practice in schools and aims to stimulate discussion about its effectiveness.

Conference publications

Papers at official conferences, seminars and meetings are more likely to be published departmentally than by HMSO. They provide information on new research or raise important current issues and stimulate professional discussion. Several departments publish complete conference proceedings from time to time, though in some cases individual papers may be published separately or only a summary of the meeting produced. Examples include *The proceedings of the prison psychologists' conference 1987* (Home Office, 1988) and *Papers presented at the seminar 'Germany rejoins the club'* (1989) from the Foreign and Commonwealth Office.

Reference sources

A number of useful reference sources and series are published departmentally and many are free of charge. They include several directories like the Department of Education and Science's *School/industry links: a directory of organisations* (rev. ed., 1987) and the annual guide to *National statistical offices of the world* from the DTI's Export Market Information Centre. The Department of the Environment/Department of Transport Library Services produced a directory of *Transport organizations in the United Kingdom* (2nd ed., 1986), while the DTI Insolvency Service issued a *List of official receivers* (1989).

Reference handbooks may be published departmentally, like the Home Office Scientific Research and Development Branch's *Scene of crime handbook of fingerprint development techniques* (1988, £5) and the *Handbook of contraceptive practice* (rev. ed., 1990) from the UK health departments. The Small Firms Service's *National reference book* is one example of an alternative to printed reference sources. Despite its title, this guide to sources of information for small businesses and their advisers is a computer database distributed on disc. Similarly the *PICKUP training directory* of training courses funded by the DES is a database available on Prestel, as well as on floppy disc, CD-ROM, microfiche and in print.

The Foreign and Commonwealth Office publishes two series which throw light on international relations. The *Background briefs* are short papers on international problems and incidents including *World population issues* (1990) and *Soviet propaganda organisations: a survey* (1989). The *Foreign policy documents* are usually more substantial and provide detailed analysis; 10−20 of these are published each year, like *The Fiji coup 1987: context and chronology* (FPD 191, 1988). The circulation of both series is controlled; they are available to the public only on microfiche from Chadwyck-Healey.

Specifications and evaluations

The government is a major purchaser of materials and equipment, particularly for defence, health services, buildings, offices and roads. In some cases it lays down its own specifications as to performance or quality standards which must be met, or it issues design guides to aid contractors. Many of the military specifications are confidential, but other kinds are publicly available. The Department of Transport issues a *Departmental standard and advice note* series on design considerations in building roads and specifications for materials like bituminous road surfaces. Government departments may also carry out evaluations of products and equipment: the Supplies Technology Division of the Department of Health issued 70 reports on medical processes and equipment in 1989, from a blood analyser to video printers.

Statistics and surveys

Despite HMSO's extensive publishing of statistics and surveys, an increasing range of figures are issued departmentally. The Rayner reviews of government statistical services in the early 1980s led to more departmental publishing of figures formerly put out by HMSO. The Welsh Office, Scottish Office and Northern Ireland departments are responsible for publishing many of their own statistics from annual abstracts for each country and *Welsh social trends* (biennial) to *Scottish sea fisheries statistical tables* (annual) and the *Environmental digest for Wales* (annual).[11] These can be produced more quickly and at lower cost than comparable HMSO statistics. The Welsh Office now issues 23 regular titles as well as one-off statistical publications; it has even produced a *Digest of Welsh historical statistics* (2 vols, 1985) with some figures going back to the 16th century. The changes at the Central Statistical Office in 1989 enlarged its own output of statistics as it took over the former DTI statistical press notices and began publishing a series of over 20 *Business bulletins* to replace figures previously appearing in *British business*.

Many government departments issue a series of statistical bulletins. The *OPCS monitors* are designed for speedy publication of the latest figures including population estimates and projections, births, deaths, marriage and divorce statistics, and figures for certain diseases. More than 20 series are published at varying frequencies and prices.[6] The Home Office also has an extensive series of statistical bulletins (46 in 1989) for figures on immigration, drowning, drunkenness, drug abuse and the probation service. The DES publishes six priced volumes of *Statistics of education* (£12 each in 1989) and a series of free statistical bulletins on such topics as further education students and pupil/teacher ratios.

Most departments also produce individual sets of figures for their subject field. The Department of Energy produces the monthly *Energy trends* giving energy production and consumption figures; the Department of the Environment figures include the occasional *Development control statistics: England* while the Overseas Development Administration publishes *British aid statistics* annually.[12] The latest figures will usually be found in press releases from departments, some issued on a regular monthly basis, and often these are the only source for the data. Not all statistics collected by government departments are published because demand may not be sufficient. The contacts listed in *Government statistics: a brief guide to sources* (free from the CSO) may be able to supply these unpublished figures.

Surveys are commissioned and published directly by departments using their own staff or consultants as well as by HMSO. A survey from the former DHSS that sounds interesting is *Alcohol related problems in undergraduate medical education: a survey of English medical schools* (1987). The Social Survey Division of the OPCS issues papers on population, survey and medical topics in their *Occasional papers* series. The Scottish Office Central Research Unit carries out special surveys like the *Edinburgh crime survey* (1990) or *Smoking in the workplace* (1989).

Historical and cultural publications

Only the occasional historical or cultural publication or guidebook is issued departmentally. To mark its 50th anniversary the Central Statistical

Office published *Keeping score* (1991), a comparison of statistics from 50 years ago with today's figures. The OPCS has produced *150 years of population and medical statistics* (1987) in its Spotlight series, while the Home Office has issued a brief *History of passports* (1989). More recent history is covered in *Telecommunications liberalisation in the UK: key elements, history and benefits* (1989) from the DTI. The Royal Commission on the Ancient and Historical Monuments of Scotland published the substantial *Catalogue of records: Scottish industrial archaeology survey 1977–85* (1990), while the *List of ancient monuments in Scotland* (1989) is put out by the Scottish Development Department.

Bibliographic and research sources

A greater number of bibliographies and other library publications are produced departmentally than by HMSO. Government department libraries are quite prolific compilers of bibliographies, literature reviews, current awareness services and research listings. Many publish bibliographies of the department's own publications (discussed in Chapter 5). Most publish regular lists of additions to the library and lists of periodicals taken. Bibliographies, reading lists and literature reviews usually appear in series or as periodicals. The Department of Agriculture and Fisheries for Scotland produces a monthly list of literature on *Salmon farming* at its Freshwater Fisheries Laboratory. The DTI Library and Information Centre's *Bibliography series* includes such titles as *Sources of information on exporting* (1990) and *Insider trading: a reading list* (1988). Some guides to the literature are issued to highlight key sources, like *Sources of information on sport and recreation* (2nd ed., 1987) from the Department of the Environment/Department of Transport Library Service.

Current awareness services include the monthly *COI Library and Information Centre bulletin* and the Department of Energy Library's *Current energy information* (weekly), which also covers forthcoming conferences and publications every fortnight. Some abstracting services are published departmentally, notably *Nursing research abstracts* (Department of Health, quarterly) and the Department of the Environment and Department of Transport *Library bulletin* (fortnightly). Computerization of government department libraries has resulted in the creation of several databases, a few of which are available to external users. The DHSS-DATA database has been available on DATASTAR for several years and includes additions to the Department of Health/Department of Social Security library.[13] It is a substantial database covering social work, social security, the health services, nursing research and preventive medicine, with about 10,000 new records added each year.

Some departments produce lists of current research projects when a regular report or list is not published through HMSO. The Home Office Research and Planning Unit's *Research programme* (annual) and its Scientific Research and Development Branch's *Fire research review* both summarize current projects and list those planned for the next year. Similarly, the *Department of Energy: offshore research and development programme: current projects* (1989) covers its extensive involvement in offshore projects. Some specialized research listings on specific topics are produced like *Acid deposition register of research in Scotland* (4th ed., 1989) from the Scottish Development Department.

Audiovisual materials
Many departments produce films, video recordings, posters, maps and other audiovisual materials to illustrate their work or as part of campaigns to inform the public. Government advertising on television has expanded greatly in the last decade with campaigns on drink and driving, cracking crime, the Single European Market and energy saving among others. These and other topics are covered in videos from departments. The DTI's European single market campaign was reinforced by two videos designed to spread the message among businesses: *Europe open for business* and *1992 — what's that?*, and by a series of posters. The Department of Employment supports its *Code of practice on the employment of disabled people* with two videos on the practical aspects of employing people with disabilities: *It can be done* and *It worked fine*. The Department of the Environment offers the video on *Buying your council home* on free loan to council and other tenants interested in exercising their right to buy. The Home Office has issued a series of posters on crime prevention and safety matters like *Got a knife? Then you've got trouble* (1988) and *It's a crime not to read it* (1988). It also produces videos like *'Getting the record straight'. Tape recording of interviews* (1988) which introduces the use of recordings in collecting evidence. Most of the films and videos are available for sale or hire from CFL Vision.

References and further reading
1   Rodgers, F., *A guide to British government publications*, New York, H. W. Wilson, 1980.

2   Fuller accounts of central government administration are given in: Hanson, A. H. and Walles, M., *Governing Britain*, 5th ed, Fontana, 1990; Hennessy, P., *Whitehall*, Secker & Warburg, 1989.

3   Barker, M., 'Who publishes official information on statistics: a personal view' in *Who publishes official information on statistics?* edited by Valerie J. Nurcombe, Library Association, Information Services Group, SCOOP, 1989, 18–23; Brittin, M., 'Overview of official statistical publishing', *ibid.*, 6–17.

4   A full discussion of the effects of the Rayner review can be found in: Allan, A., *The myth of government information*, Library Association Publishing, 1990, 12–29.

5   'The new Central Statistical Office', *Statistical news*, 85, May 1989, 4–5.

6   Burge, S., 'OPCS publications' in *Who publishes official information on health, safety and social services?* edited by Valerie J. Nurcombe, Library Association, Information Services Group, SCOOP, 1989, 21–5.

7   Englefield, D., *Whitehall and Westminster*, Longman, 1985, Appendix 3, 202–4.

8   Summaries of publishing in government departments are provided by two SCOOP seminars: Buchanan, D., 'Department of Health and Social Services publishing', 18–20; and Rowland, D., 'The Office of Fair Trading (OFT)', 48–52 in *Who publishes official information on health, safety and social services?* edited by Valerie J. Nurcombe, Library Association, Information Services Group, SCOOP, 1989. Also, 'Department of Trade and Industry, Department of Energy and associated organisations', 11–44 (7 papers) in *Who publishes official information for business and industry?* edited by Valerie J. Nurcombe, Library Association, Information Services Group, SCOOP, 1989.

9   These and other official sources relevant to community information are discussed in: Bunch, A. J., *Sources of community information*, Library Association, Branch and Mobile Libraries Group, 1986, 15–31.

10 Deft, P., 'Spearhead' in *British official publications online* edited by Valerie J. Nurcombe, Library Association, Information Services Group, SCOOP, 1990, 39–44.

11 Hills, P., 'Scottish Office' in *Who publishes official information on statistics?* Library Association, Information Services Group,

SCOOP, 1989, 62–70; Swires-Hennessy, E., 'Publishing statistics for Wales', *ibid.*, 58–61.

12 Statistical publishing in a number of central government departments is summarized in a series of papers: Keith, S., 'Department of Education and Science publications', 24–30; Shrigley, S., 'DHSS statistics: publications and sources of information', 31–42; Wishart, L., 'Home Office', 43–50; Rooney, J., 'Department of Transport statistics', 51–7 in *Who publishes official information on statistics?* edited by Valerie J. Nurcombe, Library Association, Information Services Group, SCOOP, 1989.

13 Smith, D., 'DHSS-DATA' in *British official publications online* edited by Valerie J. Nurcombe, Library Association, Information Services Group, SCOOP, 1990, 25–9.

4 *National and regional public bodies*

Public bodies proliferated from the 1940s to the 1970s as a result of increased government activity in all aspects of national life. The idea of having a government minister responsible for sport with public bodies involved in promoting it would be quite foreign to 19th or early 20th century ideas of government and its role. Yet in 1965 the Sports Council was set up, at first as an advisory body. In 1972 it became an executive body for promoting sport, supported by a series of Regional Councils for Sport and Recreation. The establishment of public bodies for specific purposes is not new however: Commissioners of Customs were first appointed in 1671 and a single Board of Customs was established in 1823. What is new is the growth in numbers of such bodies until the early 1980s and their spread into new areas of official concern.

Public bodies can be recognized because of their dependence on Parliament or the government in one or more ways. Finance is often the most tangible link as many official bodies receive funds directly or indirectly from the government. A significant number are statutory bodies set up by Act of Parliament, though they may also be established by delegated legislation or ministerial decision. The chairman and often the members of the body may be selected by a minister. Many official bodies are required to submit a regular report (usually annual) to Parliament or to the minister which permits examination of their work. Some have permanent civil service staff, in which case they are included in the *Civil Service yearbook* (HMSO, annual). A number of bodies like the BBC, the British Council and the Research Councils have a Royal Charter which gives them greater independence and sets out their purpose, constitution and powers. *Public bodies* (HMSO, annual) lists many official bodies under the sponsoring departments.[1] It also provides an analysis of their number and type since 1979 which shows a decline from 2,167 bodies then to 1,539 in 1990. This is mainly because of the abolition of many advisory bodies. Table 4 is based on the categories used in *Public bodies*, adapted to cover some research organizations and other bodies which it omits. Also included in this chapter are some of the new executive agencies (which are also omitted from *Public bodies*).

Table 4 National and regional public bodies

1. Executive bodies	┌ Nationalized industries
	├ Special purpose agencies
2. Advisory bodies	├ Regulatory bodies
	├ Consumer consultative bodies
3. Research organizations	├ Promotional organizations
	├ Development agencies
4. NHS authorities	├ Education/training bodies
	└ National museums, galleries and libraries
5. Tribunals	

The definition of official bodies varies and estimates of their number depend on the definition used. In some cases it has been restricted to executive bodies to which the government has delegated specific powers to run a service or undertaking which it felt should not be the direct responsibility of a minister or department: there are currently about 400 of these. *Public bodies* lists 'public bodies for which Ministers have a degree of accountability'. It puts their number at just under 2,000 (including NHS authorities) as it lists advisory bodies and tribunals as well as executive ones. Even so, it excludes many official research organizations and certain other bodies like the agricultural marketing boards.

Official bodies are frequently referred to in the media as 'Quangos'. This is an imprecise term and the designations 'public body' or 'official body' are preferred here. The Adam Smith Institute estimated their number at around 3,000 in 1979.[2] Several hundred were abolished in the early 1980s following a government review of their work,[3] but a substantial number of new bodies have been created since then. It is difficult to define the boundaries of 'official bodies', especially the point at which an organization receiving government funds ceases to be 'official'. The universities receive much of their current and capital finance indirectly from the government but they are not normally classified as official bodies in the UK. The groupings in Table 4 are intended to be practical rather than definitive.

Apart from the list in *Public bodies*, one of the best sources for identifying official bodies is *Councils, committees and boards* (7th ed., CBD Research, 1989). This lists bodies connected with the government in an advisory, consultative or executive capacity at national or regional level. It gives valuable information about their establishment and membership, purpose, activities and publications as well as basic names and addresses. It is useful for the majority of official bodies except tribunals and research establishments. Also useful for identifying organizations and giving details of the types of publications they issue is the *Directory of British official publications* (2nd ed., Mansell, 1984) which is discussed in the next chapter; it does not give any indication of the work of each body, however.

Keeping up-to-date with the changes in official bodies is difficult, especially as organizations may be abolished or merged and new bodies created. In April 1988 the Manpower Services Commission became the Training Commission, only to be abolished in September 1988 when it became the Department of Employment's Training Agency. After two years the name changed again to become the Department's Training, Enterprise and Education Directorate. Government departments review public bodies at least once during the life-time of each Parliament. If an organization has been abolished or a new body created since the latest issue of *Public bodies* it is often only through the newspapers or by close attention to *Hansard* that this can be ascertained. The new executive agencies set up since mid-1988 are good illustrations of this.

EXECUTIVE BODIES

Successive governments have over the years set up public bodies to which they have devolved executive powers for a special purpose. The duties and terms of reference of these bodies may be specified in an Act of Parliament, in delegated legislation or in a ministerial statement. Most have a board or council to decide policy, with a chairman responsible for the day-to-day running of the organization. The chairman and some or all of the members are appointed by a government minister, though some boards include representatives of groups interested in the topic. Executive bodies are not so confined in their actions as government departments as they are less accountable to Parliament. Their degree of autonomy varies considerably: the Chief Executive of the new executive agencies report to the parent department while organizations like the BBC are much more independent. Many executive bodies publish a substantial amount and a few are very prolific indeed: the BBC ranks among the largest commercial publishers in the country. As Table 4 shows, executive bodies may be divided into several different groups.

Nationalized industries

This group of organizations is of declining importance as the privatization of nationalized industries has been a major part of the government's programme in the 1980s. By 1990 major industries like British Airways, British Gas, British Steel, British Telecom, the regional water authorities and the regional electricity companies had been sold to shareholders. In preparation for privatization of electricity generation two generating companies, Powergen and National Power, were set up in 1990. The government intends to privatize most of the remaining nationalized industries, including British Rail and British Coal. Other bodies in this group include the Post Office, London Regional Transport, British Waterways Board and the Civil Aviation Authority. The government also holds most or all of the shares in a few organizations constituted as public companies like British Nuclear Fuels plc. Nationalized industries are still a fairly important element in the British economy employing about 2.5% of the workforce.

Most nationalized industries are constituted as public corporations with a chairman and board members appointed by a minister, like the British Railways Board which was set up under the Transport Act 1962. The staff are not civil servants and the chairman is responsible for management of the industry. Some have a regional structure or regional organizations like British Rail with Network Southeast or the London-Midland Region. Nationalized industries aim to meet government objectives for the industry and are expected to make an adequate return on the capital employed. British Rail has been set objectives covering targets for quality of service and elimination of government subsidy. Parliamentary supervision of the nationalized industries is exercised in a number of ways. The Monopolies and Mergers Commission investigates their efficiency and they are also examined by House of Commons Select Committees and the Public Accounts Committee.

Privatization has not greatly changed the publishing programmes of the former nationalized industries, but it has transferred them out of the 'official' category.[4] In discussing publishing by the remaining nationalized industries emphasis is given to those whose privatization is not imminent. Their publishing output is often extensive but may be difficult to find out about. Some kinds of publications are widely known and easily available like the rail timetables and Post Office services guides. Other items may be restricted in circulation to specific customers or are available only in small quantities. Regional divisions or organizations are often publishers in their own right. Their publications may not even be known within the national organization as the publishing system is rarely coordinated.

Each nationalized industry issues an annual report to keep the public and Parliament informed of its performance: this is usually stocked by HMSO bookshops. A short version may be issued free for a wider public like *The Post Office report and accounts 1988−89: a report to customers* (1989). Publicity material is widely circulated to promote the image of the industry and to make the public aware of its products, services and achievements. British Nuclear Fuels promotes awareness of nuclear power through booklets like *Nuclear energy: don't be left in the dark* (1988) and its *Sellafield Visitors' Centre: a window on the nuclear world* (1988). The Post Office produces comprehensive guides to postage rates and information for philatelists like the annual *Stamp Bug calendar and collectors' guide*, as well as a range of promotional leaflets including *Royal Mail is big business* (1988). Material aimed specifically at schools may be produced: British Coal offers a teachers' pack, charts and a video on coal, while the Post Office has primary and middle school packs and a range of videos for free loan.

Some nationalized industries have extensive research programmes and their own research establishments: British Coal spent over £27 million on research in 1989−90 and has two main research organizations − its Technical Department and the Coal Research Establishment. The research publications produced may be confidential and restricted to internal or controlled external circulation. Some are of wider interest like *Clean use of coal* (British Coal Corporation, 1987). Some of the research is disseminated in technical journals.

Staff need clear information on what the organization is doing and plans to do through newsletters and house journals like *Railnews* (monthly) which is free to BR employees. They may be the target for management campaigns like British Rail's energy-saving leaflet *Savers of the lost arc* (1988) from its London-Midland Region. Training manuals, films and videos provide instruction on procedures and customer relations. Because of the importance of customer relations some industries have codes of practice for standards of service and complaints procedure. The Post Office publishes *The code of practice* and monitors its performance in the quarterly *Quality of service* leaflets. Nationalized industries may issue handbooks for equipment, e.g. *Flexible trailing cables* (1989) from British Coal. A few bibliographical and research sources are produced: British Rail publishes *British Rail research. Monthly review of technical literature*, for example.

Publications lists are not always issued and those which exist may be selective like the Post Office's *A guide to helpful publications*. Coverage of nationalized industries' publications in bibliographies is sparse.

Special purpose agencies

A number of executive bodies are concerned with 'technical' services which are regarded as needing little political control. They include semi-autonomous public corporations like the BBC and the Bank of England.[5] Several of the new executive agencies, and those parts of government departments identified as potential agencies, are involved in running uncontroversial services like the Vehicle Inspectorate, the Patent Office and the Land Registry. Other bodies in this group include several concerned with the environment: the Countryside Commission, Forestry Commission and English Heritage. One of the most unusual official bodies is the Tote (the Horserace Totalisator Board), a Home Office body which runs betting at racecourses and has high street betting shops. It ploughs back its profits into racing. The Advisory, Conciliation and Arbitration Service (ACAS) is an example of an earlier generation of 'hived off' agencies which undertook functions previously carried out by government departments, removing them from direct political control as recommended by the Fulton report on the Civil Service (Cmnd.3638, 1968).

English Heritage and Cadw

English Heritage (the Historic Buildings and Monuments Commission for England) and Cadw: Welsh Historic Monuments are two executive bodies which took over the management of ancient monuments from government departments. In Scotland this was still the responsibility of the Scottish Development Department until 1991 when its Historic Buildings and Monuments Directorate became the executive agency of Historic Scotland. The Department of the Environment for Northern Ireland is responsible for 165 historic monuments there. English Heritage and Cadw also advise on which buildings should be listed as of historic interest and make grants for their repair. In publishing terms the establishment of these bodies has made acquiring their output more difficult. The guides to ancient monuments were formerly published by HMSO and were quite widely available. Now many can only be obtained at the monument itself and at a few others in the same area. English Heritage has no complete catalogue of its publications and does not even have a central point which deals with all of them.[6] Cadw is somewhat better in this respect and is at least covered in the *Catalogue of British official publications* (under the Welsh Office).

Publications cover more than just ancient monuments: English Heritage publishes a useful *Register of parks and gardens of special historic interest in England* in 44 parts while its English Heritage Technical Handbook on *Practical building conservation* (5 vols, 1988) is published commercially by Gower Technical Press. The annual *English Heritage monitor* provides statistics and indicates trends in conservation, presentation of properties, and visitors. Its *Archaeological reports* series provides scholarly accounts of sites like *Corbridge: excavations of the Roman fort and town, 1947–80* (1989). It also publishes a glossy *English Heritage magazine* (1988–, quarterly) and a substantial guide to its properties for its membership which numbers over 150,000. Since 1989 HMSO has handled some English Heritage titles as agency publications. Others are co-published commercially like the series from Batsford covering individual monuments, e.g. *Avebury* (1989), and types of monument, e.g. *Abbeys and priories* (1990). Apart from guides to individual monuments, Cadw issues a series of lists of buildings of architectural or historic interest in each town in Wales and a *Schedule of ancient monuments of national importance* for each county.

The BBC

The British Broadcasting Corporation is too well known to require any description of its main functions of providing television and national and local radio stations in the UK. Its World Service broadcasts to over 100 countries in 36 languages and is financed by government grant. The BBC is a complex organization controlled by the Director General who is in turn appointed by the board of governors. Publishing is one of the activities by which it supplements its licence income. BBC Books publishes a wide range of material related to broadcasts, including children's books, language courses, music guides, quiz books and books of the programme like Madhur Jaffrey's *Far Eastern cookery* (1989). It also sells the *BBC Radio collection* of audio cassettes ranging from *Fawlty Towers* to Shakespeare's plays. Some titles are co-published with commercial publishers like the *BBC pronouncing dictionary of British names* from Oxford University Press. Several popular periodicals are published by BBC Magazines including the *Radio times* (weekly) and *BBC wildlife* (monthly). Videos of television programmes are sold by BBC Enterprises which issues catalogues. BBC Education publications support educational broadcasts and are marketed separately; they include books and audio materials like *Getting started* (1989), the first of a series of training packs for school governors. Less well-known are the technical reports issued by the Engineering Division. The BBC has an extensive research programme on developments like high definition television and *Digital television routing systems* (BBC Report RD 1988/3). BBC Monitoring publishes daily reports of news from 130 countries worldwide and a weekly economic report, both in four parts for different regions of the world, in its *Summary of world broadcasts*, which is also available as an online database. BBC regions publish some material themselves like the *It's my city project directory* (1989) from BBC North West. Publications from BBC Books are listed in seasonal catalogues aimed at commercial booksellers and are widely available. The more specialized publications have to be acquired direct from the BBC.

The Ordnance Survey
Two bodies which are remarkable for their volume of publishing in their specialized fields are the Patent Office and the Ordnance Survey. The Ordnance Survey is Britain's official mapping body and is an executive agency. Its activities receive government financial support at present, but the eventual aim is full cost recovery despite the expense of its extensive mapping programme. It produces a wide range of current maps at scales which show the whole of Britain on two sides of a single sheet (1:625,000) to large-scale plans each covering an area 500 metres square (1:1250). A quarter of a million individual sheets are currently available.

Its best-known maps are the 1:50,000 Landranger series which covers the country in 204 sheets and reveals an immense amount of detail with great clarity. There are many larger scale maps and plans. The 1:25,000 scale Pathfinder series is useful to walkers, climbers and anglers, and for popular leisure areas like the Lake District or the New Forest there are special Outdoor leisure maps giving a wealth of tourist information. The 1:10,000 scale is the largest to cover the whole country, though the much more detailed 1:2,500 scale maps cover all parts except mountain and moorland areas and large urban areas, the latter being covered at the 1:1,250 scale. These large-scale maps are expensive to produce and require over 200,000 sheets to cover the country, yet only a handful of copies of each are sold. They are also available on microfilm, transparencies and magnetic tape. The Ordnance Survey is digitizing its maps, but this programme is unlikely to be completed before 2015. Revising large scale maps is also very time-consuming: it took nearly 40 years to complete the postwar large-scale remapping of Britain.

Ordnance Survey maps have great value as historical sources when they are no longer current and are retained by many libraries and record offices. Special historical maps with accompanying explanatory text show the main features of Britain at different periods, like the *Map of ancient Britain* (new ed., 1989). Maps are revised regularly and the thousands of new sheets each year are recorded in the monthly *Publication report*. The OS annual catalogue of maps and services illustrates each series and gives general information on availability. The Ordnance Survey has its own network of agents with large stocks of maps, and most booksellers and many newsagents have at least the more popular maps. Since 1981 the Ordnance Survey has entered into co-publishing arrangements with commercial publishers, resulting in titles like the highly successful *Motoring atlas* (annual) and the OS *Leisure guides* series published with the Automobile Association.

The Patent Office

The Patent Office is also an executive agency. It registers, examines and publishes patents which are descriptions of new inventions. Since the mid-19th century Britain has had an effective patent system to protect inventors who make public details of their inventions. Patents were formerly published only after a rigorous search to ensure originality, and the inventor was granted exclusive rights to exploit the invention for 16 years. Over 1.5 million patents were published under this system. Since 1978 each patent has been published twice: in the A series within 18 months of the application date (patent applications) and in the B series once they have been examined for originality and accepted (patent grants). Numbering of these patents began at 2,000,000. This brought Britain into line with patent systems in other European countries and protection can be extended for up to 20 years. 24,000 UK patents were published in 1989 though these were not all for British inventions. 13,750 were patent applications (A series) and the rest were patent grants (B series). A growing number of patents effective in the UK (20,000 in 1989) are granted by the European Patent Office. Each patent specification is published separately and listed in the weekly *Official journal (Patents)*. Summaries of new patents in different subject fields can be found in the 25 weekly parts of the *Abstracts of patents*, each covering a topic like organic chemistry or electronic circuits.

Information on patents is quite widely available through the Patents Information Network of public libraries in 13 towns and the British Library Science Reference and Information Service which has a virtually comprehensive collection of patents from all countries. This Network is designed to encourage greater use of the information in patents, much of which is never published in any other form. A free newsletter, *Patents information news* (quarterly), is published by the British Library to highlight the value of patents. The Patent Office also produces a useful *Introduction to patents information* (1989) which concisely explains the basics of patent documentation, as well as booklets on applying for patents and trademarks and a short video explaining its work.

Countryside Commissions

The final examples of special purpose agencies are the two Countryside Commissions, one for England and Wales and the other for Scotland. They were founded in the late 1960s to encourage and develop public recreation in the countryside and to conserve and enhance its beauty. The Commissions have designated national trails (formerly long-distance footpaths) and areas of natural beauty; they provide grants to help local authorities to establish country parks, carry out research and give advice on recreation and conservation to individuals and organizations. In the past HMSO published a number of titles for the Countryside Commission, notably the long-distance footpath guides. The Commission now co-publishes with commercial publishers and the footpath guides are glossier, if not more informative. It produces a considerable amount of material itself, including the loose-leaf *Directory of areas of outstanding natural beauty* (1989) and research reports and technical studies like *Changing river landscapes* (1987) and *Landscape assessment of farmland* (1988). Discussion documents and policy statements are issued: *Planning for change: development in a green countryside* (1988) is a topical discussion paper. Information packs offer practical help, e.g. the *Rights of way survey manual* (1988) and the *Task Force trees action pack* (1988). Two popular periodicals, *Countryside Commission news* (six a year) and *National parks today* (quarterly) are distributed free. Leaflets, posters and videos are produced for wider publicity. Publications are listed in a frequently revised catalogue put out by the Commission. The Countryside Commission for Scotland also has a substantial publishing programme and has co-published the ambitious *An inventory of gardens and designed landscapes in Scotland* (1987) in five volumes.

Regulatory bodies

A significant minority of executive bodies exist to control and regulate an activity or industry. Some have been established as government departments, notably the Office of Gas Supply (Ofgas), the Office of Electricity Regulation (OFFER), the Office of Water Services, and the Office of Telecommunications (Oftel) which regulate the privatized industries, but most are non-departmental bodies. They have been appointed to control major concerns like health and safety, mergers, broadcasting, data protection and gambling. More specialized regulatory bodies include the British Hallmarking Council, which supervises the assay offices and enforces laws relating to hallmarking, and the Crofters Commission, which controls crofting in Scotland. In some cases an organization has both regulatory and promotional roles like the Equal Opportunities Commission and the Commission for Racial Equality. The Civil Aviation Authority (reclassified as a nationalized industry in *Public bodies*) is essentially a regulatory body. The number of regulatory bodies is growing as new ones are established like the National Rivers Authority which sets and monitors water quality standards and the Radio Authority which supervises independent radio.

Several statutory bodies regulate individual professions, especially those concerned with medicine. These bodies are concerned with standards of professional education and training, keep a register of qualified practitioners and take disciplinary action in cases of professional misconduct and negligence. The General Medical Council, the General Optical Council and the Architects' Registration Council were all established by Act of Parliament and a proportion of Council members are Crown appointees. Their publications include annual reports, a register of professionals like the *Medical register* (General Medical Council, annual), pamphlets and regulations on education, training and registration, and sometimes training materials. These are published directly by the organizations concerned.

The publications of some major regulatory bodies like the Monopolies and Mergers Commission and the Audit Commission are mostly produced by HMSO (q.v.). In cases like the Health and Safety Commission and Executive the main publications are issued by HMSO but there are a considerable number of direct publications as well. Other regulatory bodies issue a larger proportion of their publications themselves. Only the annual accounts of the Commission for Racial Equality (CRE) is published by HMSO. The Equal Opportunities Commission (EOC) publishes its main research series through HMSO, as well as annual reports and accounts, but most other material is non-HMSO.

Regulatory bodies produce quite a wide variety of publications. Apart from annual reports, they normally explain their role in leaflets like the EOC's *What we are. What we do. How we can help you.* They may publish the legislation they enforce or explanations of its effects. Guidance on observing the regulations is provided, like *Avoiding sex bias in selection testing: guidance for employers* (EOC, 1988). They may investigate alleged infringements, like the CRE's *Medical school admissions: report of a formal investigation into St. George's Medical School* (1988), or publish the decisions of court cases. Some regulatory bodies issue consultation documents: in 1988 the Data Protection Registrar produced *What are your views? Monitoring and assessment of the Data Protection Act 1984.* They advise the government on the effects of its policies and may propose new measures: the EOC made comments on *National testing and equal opportunities* (1987) to the Department of Education and Science and submitted proposals on *Equal treatment of men and women: strengthening the act* (1988). They carry out relevant research and undertake surveys like the Civil Aviation Authority (CAA)'s *Business air fares: a UK survey* (1988) and *Smoke hoods: net safety benefits* (1987). The CAA is one of the regulatory bodies which is responsible for assessment of practitioners: it publishes examination syllabuses and training manuals for pilots, navigators and air traffic controllers. A regular newsletter or journal like the CRE's *New community* (three a year) or the *HSC newsletter* (Health and Safety Commission, six a year) provides up-to-date information about events, developments, research and issues. Statistics are collected to monitor the activity and may be published: the EOC produces current statistics about equality in the annual *Women and men in Britain: a statistical profile*, while the CAA publishes the alarming *UK airmiss statistics.* Many of the regulatory bodies issue a publications list.

The Health and Safety at Work Act 1974 established both the Health and Safety Commission (HSC) and the Health and Safety Executive (HSE) to develop health and safety policies and ensure enforcement of the legislation.[7] The HSC is advised by committees for different industries and for subjects like toxic substances and genetic manipulation. The HSE includes government inspectors of the Factory Inspectorate and for nuclear installations, mines and quarries, etc. Its Employment Medical Advisory Service provides an advice service on work-related illnesses. HSC/HSE together produce a large number of publications. The great majority of priced publications are from HMSO, notably the five series of *Guidance notes* and the *Health and safety booklets*. New regulations, codes of practice and studies are also published by HMSO. Non-HMSO publications include several series of free leaflets dealing with specific types of hazards like the *Agricultural safety* series on *Cyanide gassing powders* (1986) or *Safety with chain saws* (1986). The *Technical information leaflets* cover a range of issues from respiratory apparatus and explosions to environmental contaminants. The main priced publications are in the *Methods for the determination of hazardous substances* series. HSC/HSE issue a number of journals like *Site safe news* (two a year, free) and the *Toxic substances bulletin* (two a year, priced). The largest quantity of non-HMSO publications from HSE is its *Translations series*, in which several hundred titles appear each year. HSE also produce films and other audiovisual materials to publicize safety hazards. Details of HSE publications are available in printed lists and on Prestel. They are also included with other literature on health and safety matters in the HSELINE database and OSH-ROM, a collection of three major international health and safety databases on CD-ROM.

The Commission for Racial Equality was set up as a statutory body in 1976 under the Race Relations Act 1976 to eliminate discrimination and promote equality of opportunity and good race relations. It keeps the working of the legislation under review and has investigative powers when individuals or organizations are believed to be contravening the act. It will also help individuals complaining of discrimination. Like the EOC, it issues a series of publications to explain the legislation and to offer guidance to employers, employees, local authorities and others e.g. *Race, housing and immigration: a guide* (1989). It has issued codes of practice on racial discrimination at work and a guide for trainers on implementing equal opportunities policies. The CRE's main journal is *New community* (three a year) which reports on research and discusses current issues. It carries out surveys on aspects of discrimination like *Ethnic minority school teachers: a survey in eight local education authorities* (1988) and publishes papers of conferences and seminars, e.g. *Britain: a plural society* (1990). The CRE believes in developing understanding of the cultures of the different ethnic minorities in Britain through publications like *The Shap handbook on world religions in education* (1987) which it co-published. The majority of its publications are now priced. CRE titles are listed in the *Home Office list of publications* (annual).

Consumer consultative bodies

Consumers' interests are represented to government through the National Consumer Council and a number of consultative bodies. These concentrate on services provided by current and former nationalized industries. There are nearly 40 national and area councils and committees covering electricity, gas, coal, water, transport, telecommunications and the Post Office. These are all established as executive bodies, but the Community Health Councils which represent the views of health service users in each District Health Authority are advisory.

The consumers' councils are independent of the industry concerned. Several advise the Director General of one of the regulatory agencies overseeing a privatized industry, like the Customer Services Committees for the water industry. Area committees like the Midlands Regional Electricity Consumers' Committee include representatives of local authorities and local consumers. They are a forum for consumers' problems and views and also carry out their own reviews and investigations of the quality of service provided. Publications are usually issued direct and few councils have publications lists. Most publish an annual report listing their membership and reviewing their work, together with publicity leaflets to make the public aware of their existence. Some councils issue advisory pamphlets, newsletters and investigative reports on the industry. The Post Office Users' National Council has published more than most other consultative bodies with 45 reports between 1970 and 1990 on increases in postal charges and the efficiency of the postal services, like its annual *Customer audit and review of the Post Office* and *Queuing for service: Post Office compared with others* (1989). Its newsletter, *POUNC news*, appears irregularly.

The National Consumer Council (NCC) was set up in 1975 to identify consumers' interest and to ensure that they are represented to government, businesses and the professions. Separate Consumer Councils for Scotland and Wales work closely with the NCC. It undertakes campaigns on strengthening the rights of consumers, for instance by reforming sale of goods legislation and making the court system more accessible. Unlike the consultative councils, it does not deal with individual consumer complaints. A few titles are published for the NCC by HMSO, but most of its books, policy papers and periodicals are published directly. *Consumer voice* (quarterly) is its main journal with news and articles about current concerns and campaigns. Several books aimed at consumers, educators and officials are published each year. These include the *Consumer Congress directory* (8th ed., 1988) covering over 200 consumer organizations; sets of guidelines like *Open to complaints* (1988) on social services complaints procedures; action guides like *Pedestrians* (1987) which aims to improve conditions for those on foot; and reports and surveys like *Home truths: consumers' experiences of moving house in England and Wales* (1990). The NCC policy papers series publishes its comments and responses on government policies and proposals: 35 were published in 1987, including *Tenant's choice: response to the DoE* and *Supply of beer, response to Monopolies and Mergers Commission*. Most publications except the annual reports are priced and a publications catalogue is issued.

Promotional organizations

Many official bodies promote a particular activity, interest or area which the government considers significant and worth encouraging. These organizations act as a focus for activities in the field but the nature of their involvement in promotion varies. Some are grant-making organizations providing finance to encourage an activity, others are more concerned with promoting sound policies in their field, while some are producers' organizations marketing a product. Most promotional bodies have a central organization with in some cases a regional structure like the regional arts or tourist boards. Several have separate organizations for different parts of the UK, like the Scottish and Welsh Arts Councils, but some act for the UK as a whole. Publications are obviously important in promotional work and a wide range of material is issued centrally. The regions may have their own independent publishing programmes. There may also be cooperation with commercial publishers: British Council publications are issued by several commercial publishers and by HMSO as well as by the Council itself.

General promotional bodies

A number of important general promotional bodies like the British Council, the Sports Council and the Design Council offer a wide range of information and publications. The British Council promotes knowledge of Britain and the English language abroad, with particular emphasis on culture and education. It has offices and libraries in over 80 countries. Its publications are useful in Britain as well as abroad and include reference works like the annual guide to *Studying and living in Britain* for overseas students and *Scholarships abroad* for British students. Both are published for the Council by Northcote House and HMSO respectively. The British Council's own publications include market surveys of English language teaching in selected countries, the Nexus series of studies of Commonwealth writers in English, and exhibition catalogues of British art like *Cries and whispers* (1989), the enigmatically-titled catalogue of contemporary art purchased for the British Council collection during the 1980s. It also publishes the invaluable *British book news* (monthly) which reviews several thousand new British books a year. The British Council produces audiovisual materials both on its own and with other publishers, especially to support English language teaching. Its three *Briefing on Britain* videos are available in three versions for students in the Middle East and Far East. The British Council's publications catalogue includes the titles available from other publishers.

The Design Council and the Crafts Council promote design and craftsmanship in Britain. They maintain indexes of well-designed products and of craftsmen, organize exhibitions, and issue the periodicals *Design* and *Engineering*, both monthly from the Design Council, and *Crafts* (bi-monthly). The Design Council publishes books and catalogues on design management, design history, design engineering and design education, like the annual directory of *Design courses in Britain* or the study of *British Rail design* (1988).

The tourist organizations have become much more forceful promoters now that tourism is a major industry with earnings of around £6,850 million from over 17 million overseas visitors to Britain in 1989. Four main statutory bodies promote tourism: the British Tourist Authority (BTA) which is responsible for the overseas promotion of tourism in Britain, and the English, Scottish and Wales Tourist Boards. Regional Tourist Boards also exist within England. Restructuring in 1990 led to more devolution of functions from ETB to the regions in England while in Wales some services are now provided by the private sector. Publication of tourist guides and other material is being contracted out. Many free and priced publications are issued for promotion and information. Magazines like *In Britain* (BTA, monthly) give details of current events. Books and pamphlets include accommodation guides, lists of restaurants, general guidebooks on what to do and see, and guides for special interests like angling, activity holidays or industrial archaeology. Brochures like *England holidays* (English Tourist Board, annual) or *Year round holidays in Wales* (Wales Tourist Board, annual) together with maps, posters and videos aim to entice the tourist. The other main group of publications is for people in the holiday industry. This includes statistics and surveys, e.g. *Tourism intelligence quarterly* (BTA), the English Tourist Board's *Horwath/ETB English hotel occupancy survey* (monthly), and the annual *Overseas visitor survey* (BTA). Tourism development publications like the BTA's *Strategy for growth 1989–93* (1989) or the Wales Tourist Board's *Inland water in Wales: development opportunities for tourism, recreation and sport* (1985) and reports like *The Channel Tunnel: will Britain's tourism industry and infrastructure be ready for 1993?* (BTA, 1989) draw attention to the need for planning. Research is carried out and advisory material issued, like *Thanks: for bringing it to my attention ...*, the Scottish Tourist Board's guide to customer relations. Many of the promotional publications are available at local tourist information centres. Each national tourist board issues a publications list, but few of the regional tourist boards do so.

Grant-making organizations

The Arts Council of Great Britain is one of a number of bodies channelling government grants to non-official organizations. Such intermediaries are essential to the government to distribute funds in an informed and effective way. At the same time they allow the recipients to retain their autonomy so that they are not directly dependent on central government. The five Research Councils receive funds to support pure and applied research in their field; their work is discussed in the section on research organizations.

The Arts Council was established in 1946 to promote the development of the arts and to make them accessible to a wider public. It makes grants to opera, ballet and theatre companies and orchestras and to individual artists and groups. Accessibility of the arts is encouraged by grants to festivals and touring companies and by the provision of travelling exhibitions. The Scottish and Welsh Arts Councils receive block grants from the Arts Council for distribution in their countries, while Northern Ireland has its own independent Arts Council. Support is also given to the regional arts boards which promote the arts within England and Wales. Arts organizations are encouraged to obtain additional funds through sponsorship by companies and grants from local authorities.

Publications are an important means of promoting awareness of arts matters and providing information for arts administrators. Arts Council publications include reference works like the *Arts centres in the United Kingdom directory* (1989) and the *Local arts councils directory* (1988), reports like *Towards cultural diversity* (1989) which monitors the Council's Ethnic Minority Arts Action Plan, and practical guides like *Dance pack* (1988). It also issues a series of briefing notes on cultural policy in different countries, guides to its awards, and studies like *The arts: politics, power and the purse* (1987) which looks at the structure of arts funding internationally. The Arts Council's annual report provides a good summary of its work, while *The insider* (quarterly) offers current news, articles and comment from the Arts Council for arts managers.

The regional arts boards have greater responsibilities than the previous regional arts associations following the Wilding Report on the structure of arts funding in 1989. They publish independently and some also have bookshops. Most issue a newsletter with details of arts events, news and grants like *Event* (ten a year) from South East Arts. They may support writing within the region: West Midlands Arts publishes the periodical *People to people* (three a year), over 20,000 copies of which are distributed free. With publishing carried out by 13 boards in England and Wales it is not always easy to trace publications, especially as they are not listed in CoBOP.

Marketing bodies

Official bodies have been set up to control and promote the marketing of agricultural produce. They include the Meat and Livestock Commission (MLC), the Potato Marketing Board, and the Apple and Pear Development Council. Marketing is usually centralized and producers may be registered. The organization may recommend prices and run advertising campaigns like those for meat. Several carry out research to improve production techniques, quality and marketing, and study the consumption and use of the product.

Publications include annual reports, publicity to encourage use of the product like *Different methods of cooking potatoes*, a factsheet from the Potato Marketing Board (1987), or the colourful *All about meat* from the MLC, and periodicals for producers, e.g. the MLC's *Meat demand trends* (three a year). Material is also produced for schools, like the information pack *Food − a focus for study* from the Milk Marketing Board. There are reports of research like the *Survey of potato research in the United Kingdom* (Potato Marketing Board, annual) and reference works like the MLC's loose-leaf *British meat export manual*. All publications are issued directly by each body, the majority of which provide a publications list.

Development agencies

Government programmes and the European Regional Development Fund have put considerable emphasis on economic and industrial regeneration and infrastructure development. The government has set up a range of agencies to promote development, usually in partnership with local businesses and local authorities. The new towns, 32 of which were designated in the UK from 1946, were early examples. Growth was planned by development corporations for each town, but these programmes are nearing completion and the Commission for the New Towns is to take over the remaining responsibilities in England. Eleven Urban Development Corporations have been set up more recently to regenerate the London docklands,[8] Merseyside, Teeside and other disadvantaged areas. English Estates is a government agency which develops and manages small factories and workshops at over 500 locations throughout the country. Development in Scotland and Wales is coordinated by Scottish Enterprise (formerly the Scottish Development Agency) and the Welsh Development Agency (WDA). Rural development is also encouraged through the Rural Development Commission in England, the WDA and the Development Board for Rural Wales, and Highlands and Islands Enterprise. Development extends beyond the UK through the Commonwealth Development Corporation and the Commonwealth Fund for Technical Co-operation which provide Commonwealth developing countries with assistance.

Highlands and Islands Enterprise (until 1991 the Highlands and Islands Development Board) is responsible for economic development in much of northern Scotland.[9] It encourages tourism and all kinds of industry and offers loans and grants for industrial or agricultural projects. In 1991 it assumed responsibility for employment training as well. Its publications programme is quite varied and only its annual accounts are published by HMSO. It produces a fair amount of tourist literature like *Crofting life holidays* (1990) but also a survey of *Expenditure of skiers at Cairngorm and Glencoe* (1986). Directories include a *Guide to Regions, Islands and District Councils* (new ed., 1990) and the *Fish farming: supplies and services directory* (1990). It issues information packs for local businesses and details of industrial sites and premises. There is even a calendar of livestock auction sales and a list of fish processing courses.

A broader economic development organization almost completely ignored in *Britain: an official handbook* is the National Economic Development Council (NEDC).[10] It is a rare meeting point for government, management and unions and aims to promote economic growth. It is concerned not only with broad economic problems but has a series of working parties and sector groups for individual industries like clothing, electronics and pharmaceuticals. They concentrate on overcoming obstacles to growth and especially on improving the performance of smaller companies, The National Economic Development Office (NEDO) provides the secretariat for the Council and its working groups. NEDO publishes about 150 titles a year, almost all directly. Its reports are analytical and topical: *Switching on skills: new approaches to skill shortages in electronics and IT* (1989) from its Electronics Industry Sector Group highlighted a growing problem, while *UK packaging – food for thought* (1989) deals with the trade deficit in food packaging and its implications for the packaging industry. The Council (NEDC) publishes a series of papers on issues of current concern, e.g. *United Kingdom trade performance* (1990). A few NEDO/NEDC publications are issued by HMSO or in association with commercial publishers, like *Women managers: the untapped resource* published by Kogan Page in 1990. HMSO has issued *The innovation management tool kit* (1990) for NEDO, a self-assessment package for industry to help identify strengths, weaknesses, opportunities and threats. NEDO issues an annual publications catalogue and most of its publications are priced, often modestly since it wants them to reach as wide an audience as possible.

Education and training bodies

A significant group of executive bodies are concerned with education and training at all levels. They include organizations which examine and offer qualifications in a wide range of subjects like the Business and Technician Education Council (BTEC) and the Council for National Academic Awards (CNAA). More specialized qualifications are offered by the Central Council for Education and Training in Social Work and the Fire Services Examinations Board. In schools the School Examinations and Assessment Council replaced the Secondary Examinations Council in 1988 as the body supervising the examination and assessment system in England and Wales. The introduction of the national curriculum is being promoted by the National Curriculum Council (for England) and the Curriculum Council for Wales. Some organizations like the Further Education Unit and the National Council for Educational Technology (NCET) support educational development. NCET was formed in 1988 following the merger of the Council for Educational Technology and the Microelectronics Education Support Unit to evaluate new technologies and their applications in education and to provide advice and support materials for teachers.

The Council for National Academic Awards was established by Royal

Charter in 1964, originally to award degrees and diplomas for courses in polytechnics and colleges. Its role now is more concerned with safeguarding standards in higher education, and validating degrees and courses for those institutions without their own degree-awarding powers. Publications are important in ensuring that standards are known and new developments communicated. The CNAA publishes regular directories of its first degree and postgraduate courses and institutions offering them. The CNAA *Handbook* (annual) lays down the principles and requirements for course approval. Several periodical titles cover news, developments and current issues: *CNAA Higher education news* (three a year) is widely circulated while the *Information Services digest* (three a year) reviews new publications relevant to higher education. Discussion papers deal with current issues like *How shall we assess them?* (1989) and shorter briefing papers keep staff up to date with developments, e.g. *Access courses to higher education* (1989). Surveys, reviews and results of research are published in a series of Development Services publications like *Accessibility of higher education* (1990). All publications are available from the CNAA Publications Unit and are listed in a frequently updated catalogue.

Industrial training is one of the areas most affected by government policy changes. At the beginning of the 1980s it was centrally led and funded, dominated by the Manpower Services Commission (MSC) and the 24 statutory industrial training boards (ITBs) for each main industry. These were financed by a levy on employers to provide training courses and facilities. By 1990 the MSC (later Training Commission) had been abolished and its role taken over by the Department of Employment's Training Agency (which became the Training, Enterprise and Education Directorate at the end of 1990), while most of the ITBs had been replaced by over 100 voluntary Industrial Training Organizations which are employer-led. These are concerned with setting standards and reviewing skill requirements in their industry. A network of 82 privately run Training and Enterprise Councils in England and Wales are responsible for providing actual training and managing the Employment Training and Youth Training programmes and other employment initiatives at local level. These replace the former Training Agency's area offices and are responsible for the £2,500 million training budget. Scottish Enterprise and Highlands and Islands Enterprise oversee training in Scotland and work through a network of local enterprise companies. In Northern Ireland the Training and Employment Agency, an executive agency within the Department of Economic Development for Northern Ireland, is responsible for training and employment services.

The Training, Enterprise and Education Directorate (TEED) promotes training, encourages enterprise and supervises the arrangements for training and vocational education. Publications are an essential part of its work and range from leaflets to make people aware of the opportunities, e.g. *Why training matters* (1988) to annual reference works like *Occupations* and the *Open learning directory* which gives details of courses in open learning format. TEED supports research and publishes studies like *Admissions to higher education: policy and practice* (1989) and produces handbooks to assist the implementation of its training programmes like *Ensuring quality in open learning: a handbook for action* (1989). Its Careers and Occupational Information Centre produces videos, e.g. the *Careers in focus* series, and multi-media packs like *Learning to listen* (1990), as well as printed careers material.

Although most statutory industrial training boards will have been wound up by 1992, two will remain in existence for construction and engineering construction. ITBs have published useful training materials, journals and newsletters, careers information, statistics, and research reports and studies.

National museums, galleries and libraries

The government provides grants to the national museums, art galleries and libraries to preserve the nation's cultural and intellectual heritage, to encourage scholarly investigation and to promote a widespread appreciation of human achievement. These bodies have extensive collections of books, manuscripts, paintings, sculptures, machines, and specimens of artistic, historical, scientific, archaeological and intellectual interest. Most have boards of trustees to decide policy and are financed mainly by the government for running costs and purchase grants. They include the British Museum, the National Gallery, the National Portrait Gallery, the Victoria and Albert Museum, the Science Museum, the Imperial War Museum and the National Museum of Wales. Museums and galleries run by local authorities, educational bodies, societies and private owners are not included in this discussion.

Museum and gallery publishing

Museums and galleries are prolific publishers of both scholarly and popular material in a variety of formats.[11] A small proportion of this material is published by HMSO, but most is issued directly or in association with commercial publishers. Most publish a guidebook, often a concise edition in several languages and a fuller edition in English only. There may be an attractive separate guide for children. Catalogues of the permanent collections, or of particular parts of them, with a description of each exhibit, are essential to scholars. The National Gallery issues a complete catalogue of its collection while in 1988 the Tate Gallery began publishing a series of substantial catalogues covering its British collection with *The age of Hogarth: British painters born 1675–1709* (1988). Catalogues of new acquisitions are usually published periodically, and briefer details of these are given in the annual reports.

All museums and galleries hold temporary exhibitions, usually with accompanying catalogues. They are publicized in free newsletters and leaflets like *Preview* (1990–, three a year) from the Tate Gallery. A few catch the public imagination and achieve large sales. Catalogues in their most abbreviated form provide a brief introduction to the subject of the exhibition, a list of exhibits and perhaps some illustrations. Many catalogues are much more substantial with a lengthy introduction, detailed notes on each exhibit and profuse illustration. Some develop into monographs on their subject: the Tate Gallery's exhibition of *The paintings of David Jones* (1989) became a book published by John Taylor and Lund Humphries with a biographical essay by Nicolette Gray and reproductions in colour of many of his paintings.

Brief illustrated booklets on many aspects of museum and gallery collections appear in profusion for the interested child or adult reader. Most have a short but systematic introduction to the topic and a selection of illustrations, often in colour. The majority are reasonably priced to attract the casual buyer and many are published in series. *The Victoria and Albert Museum colour books* are published commercially by Webb & Bower/Michael Joseph in association with the V & A. Titles include *Japanese stencils* (1988) and *Decorative endpapers* (1985). The Tate Gallery publishes a small series of colour books itself on artists like Blake, Constable and Turner. The British Museum has an extensively illustrated series of *Introductory guides* ranging from *Medieval decorative art* (1991) to *Egyptian mummies* (1984). Several museums produce material for schools: the British Museum (Natural History) has a large number of worksheets, booklets and charts, and even plastic scale models of dinosaurs.

At a more scholarly level museums and galleries may publish essays, monographs, studies and reference works usually involving research based on their collections. Essays by scholars from several different viewpoints are a useful way of examining a topic, as in the Tate's critical study of *Late Picasso 1953−1973* (1988). Essays on a theme or on a series of separate topics may appear in yearbooks like the *Imperial War Museum review* with articles on all aspects of 20th-century warfare, or in periodicals from the museum or gallery. Specialized research studies may be issued in book form, like the monumental work on *The Sutton Hoo ship burial* (three vols, 1975−83) from the British Museum or as research papers in series. The British Museum (Natural History) publishes several series of its *Bulletin*, each issue of which is a research paper on an aspect of botany, entomology, zoology or geology. Catalogues of collections, e.g. the *Catalogue of Egyptian antiquities in the British Museum* (seven vols, 1968−87), act as reference sources for identification purposes, but these are supplemented by reference works like *Principal coins of the Romans* (three vols, 1978−81), both from British Museum Press.

Many museums and galleries publish large numbers of postcards and slides offering good quality reproductions of exhibits at reasonable prices. Outstanding works may be available in faithful facsimile reproductions: prints of paintings and drawings, casts of sculptures and models of other objects.

Most museums and galleries publish in their own right and a few through HMSO, but increasingly they co-publish with a commercial publisher to achieve wider distribution through the book trade. Examples from the Tate Gallery and the V & A have already been mentioned. The National Gallery has joined with the art publisher Phaidon to publish several books related to its collections including *More than meets the eye* (1988) and *Flemish paintings* (1988).

The British Library
The British Library was set up in 1973 as the national library and the hub of the country's library and information network. It operates through three main divisions: Humanities and Social Sciences; Science, Technology and Industry, which includes the Document Supply Centre at Boston Spa; and Bibliographic Services. There is also a Research and Development Department which is a substantial publisher. Each division and section issues newsletters or journals. Many valuable bibliographic sources appear in different formats: in print, microform, CD-ROM discs and as online databases. These include the *British national bibliography* (weekly), the *General catalogue of printed books* and *British reports, translations and theses* (monthly). All three are available as online files on the British Library's BLAISE-LINE service.

The Humanities and Social Sciences division publishes catalogues of its collections of manuscripts, maps, newspapers, music and oriental material. The Science, Technology and Industry division produces reference works like the frequently updated *Guide to libraries and information units in government departments and other organisations* (29th ed., 1990) and guides to information sources on *Market research* (6th ed., 1989) or *Trade marks* (1990). It also issues useful journals like *Science and technology policy* (six a year), and the *Environment and industry digest* (monthly) which began publication in 1990. The Research and Development Department issues several report series on British Library-funded projects.

At a more popular level the British Library produces a series of paperback introductions to aspects of its collections, including *Stamps* (1987), *Books of Hours* (1985), and *Japanese book illustration* (1988). It has issued sound recordings of music from other cultures and of bird songs from the National Sound Archive collection. A range of free leaflets and booklets are provided to publicize the collections and to assist users, e.g. *A brief guide to some libraries in London* (rev. ed., 1987) and *United States government publications* (1990). An annual catalogue of British Library publications is produced, though it does not include the free guides to services. The national libraries for Scotland and Wales have their own publishing programmes, though they are much less prolific than the British Library.

ADVISORY BODIES

This is by far the largest group of public bodies numerically, though their output of publications is considerably less than for executive bodies. Advisory bodies act as a link between the government and various interest groups. They allow government departments and executive bodies to assess outside reactions to their policies and plans and to obtain expert advice from people closely involved in the field. The Health and Safety Commission's seven subject advisory committees and 11 industry advisory committees for specific industries are examples of this. Consultation with advisory bodies is a regular part of the government's decision-making process before policies are finalized.

These bodies are quite distinct from the temporary departmental committees and working parties which are set up to investigate a topic and disbanded once their report has been produced. Provision for setting up advisory bodies may be included in the relevant legislation if consultation is seen as essential, in which case they are statutory bodies.

The majority are appointed at the discretion of the minister, however. Most are standing organizations meeting fairly regularly on a continuing basis. The government regularly reviews the role of each advisory body and in 1989 there were 500 fewer than in 1979. Unlike executive bodies these organizations spend relatively little: membership is voluntary with the chairman and members normally receiving only their expenses. A few have a paid secretariat.

There are just under a thousand advisory bodies, many of them very specialized or technical. Four departments each have over 100 advisory bodies (the Department of Employment, Home Office, Lord Chancellor's Department and the Scottish Office) while others have fewer than ten (Education and Science, Transport). Examples, with the department they advise, include the Royal Fine Art Commission (Environment), the Committee on the Safety of Medicines (Health), the Retail Prices Index Advisory Committee (Employment) and the Place Names Advisory Committee (Welsh Office). Important advisory bodies include the Law Commission and Scottish Law Commission which review the law and recommend simplification or reform, and the Advisory Council on Science and Technology (Cabinet Office) which advises the Prime Minister on national priorities in research of all kinds. Some advisory bodies are constituted for Britain as a whole, but others are established for individual countries or local areas. The Scottish Office and the Welsh Office each have their own advisory bodies, while local organizations include the 122 Parole Boards and Local Review Committees advising the Home Office.

Publications of advisory bodies may be issued by HMSO: some annual reports are required by Parliament while others are published at the discretion of the minister and are usually non-parliamentary publications. Significant reports and studies published by HMSO for advisory bodies include the Law Commission reports (parliamentary) and consultation papers (non-parliamentary) and the *Food surveillance papers* (30 by 1990) of the Steering Group on Food Surveillance. The majority of reports of Health and Safety Commission advisory committees are also published by HMSO. Publishing by many of the other advisory bodies is limited: the vast majority do not even publish an annual report (though they may submit one to the minister).

Among the few which do publish their own annual reports are the Committee on the Review of Medicines, the Advisory Committee on Novel Foods and Processes, and the Historic Buildings Council for Wales. Some of the more important non-HMSO publishers among advisory bodies are the three Local Government Boundary Commissions (for England, Scotland and Wales) which issue a series of reports reviewing boundaries and electoral arrangements. A few Law Commission publications are non-HMSO, notably the quarterly *Law under review* which lists all current law revision projects. The DTI's Innovation Advisory Board produced a report on *Innovation and growth* (1990) comparing civil research and development expenditure in Britain with that abroad. A number of Department of Health and Department of Social Security advisory bodies also produce reports and periodicals, like the Committee on the Safety of Medicines' irregular newsletter *Current problems* and the Manpower Planning Advisory Group's substantial research project on *Midwives' perceptions on the state of midwifery* (1987). *Councils, committees and boards* (7th ed., CBD Research, 1989) is useful both for identifying the role of advisory bodies and indicating their main publications. Details of individual publications are often best sought in the publications list of the sponsoring department.

The Inland Waterways Amenity Advisory Council (IWAAC) was set up under the 1968 Transport Act to advise the Secretary of State for the Environment and the British Waterways Board on the recreational development of the waterways. The Council includes representatives of groups interested in the waterways: anglers, boaters, walkers, conservationists, local authorities and MPs. It meets regularly and reports to the Department and the Board; it also advises local planning authorities on issues affecting waterways locally. Like many advisory bodies, its role has been questioned in government reviews of public bodies and it narrowly escaped abolition. IWAAC issues its publications directly. They include summaries of topics discussed at its Council meetings and reports on aspects of the waterways, e.g. *Waterway architecture: an economic return from conservation* (1985). It is concerned with *Safety on the waterways* (1988) and has advised on *Marketing the waterway heritage* (1987). Its work is outlined in the *IWAAC user's pack*, but its newsletter *IWAAC news* has not been produced for some time because of staff shortages.

RESEARCH ORGANIZATIONS

Direct government support for research and development accounts for nearly 40% of research expenditure in this country. In addition, research not funded directly by the government is carried out by some nationalized industries and other public bodies like the Forestry Commission which has two research stations. *Britain: an official handbook* (HMSO, annual) provides a convenient summary of scientific research in its chapter on 'Promotion of science and technology'. The government's research budget, currently around £5,000 million a year, is spent in a number of ways. As might be expected, the Ministry of Defence is the largest single recipient, taking almost 50% of the budget for defence research and development. Overall responsibility for civil science lies with the Department of Education and Science, which funds the research councils and provides grants for other bodies like the Royal Society.

Each government department is involved with research work related to its functions: the Department of Trade and Industry has special responsibility for technological research and receives almost 10% of the budget. Some research work takes place within government departments (the Home Office Research and Planning Unit is an example) but much is undertaken on a customer-contractor basis. The government department is the customer with a research requirement and pays the research organization for the specific project instead of supporting research establishments through annual grants. Research on this basis may be carried out in government research establishments like the Transport and Road Research Laboratory, through the research councils, by industrial research organizations and professional bodies, or by teams in academic institutions. Alternatively research may be commissioned from commercial consultants who report back to the department.

The customer-contractor basis is satisfactory for much applied research but is less suited to pure research or academic investigation. The five research councils support a considerable amount of pure as well as applied research. Their annual budget is nearly £900 million which is divided unequally, about half going to the Science and Engineering Research Council. The Medical Research Council receives a fifth of the funds, the Natural Environment RC gets 15%, the Agricultural and Food RC just under 10%, while the Economic and Social RC receives only 4%. Each research council supports research units or establishments with full-time staff working on a range of investigations. The Medical Research Council [12] has over 50 research units while the Science and Engineering Research Council (SERC) supports four major establishments: the Royal Greenwich Observatory, the Royal Observatory, Edinburgh, the Daresbury Laboratory and the Rutherford Appleton Laboratory. Most of the councils also make grants to individual research workers and teams in universities and polytechnics and offer postgraduate research awards to enable students to gain experience of research.

Government support for research is so extensive that a range of publications is needed to keep track of current projects and completed research. Many research bodies issue reports on current research or registers of projects (those issued by HMSO and by government departments were mentioned in Chapter 3) including the Economic and Social Research Council's annual *Research supported by the ESRC* with summaries of each project. Ongoing research in academic institutions is listed in *Current research in Britain* (four vols, British Library, annual) which is also available online from Pergamon Financial Data Services. Newsletters and periodicals put out by the funding body may also record current work. These sources all help to avoid unnecessary duplication of research work and allow others interested in a project to contact those responsible.

Publishing pattern

The main publications from research organizations are the details of completed research. Much defence research work is secret and reports are available only to authorized users through the Defence Research Information Centre. Others are publicly available only on microfiche from Chadwyck-Healey, including titles in the Royal Aerospace Establishment's *Technical report* and *Technical memorandum* series. Ministry of Defence research establishments like the Royal Signals and Radar Establishment are increasingly working with industry and encouraging civil applications of research. This has increased the amount of research published and this trend has been strengthened by the creation of an executive agency in 1991 covering four of the non-nuclear defence research establishments.

Civil research may be published in several different ways. The sponsoring government department may publish it, either directly or through HMSO. The organization carrying out the work may publish its own series of research reports, like those of the UK Atomic Energy Authority or the Transport and Road Research Laboratory. These are usually available direct from the organization, though in a few cases HMSO acts as agent for their sale (notably the Atomic Energy Research Establishment and Culham Laboratory reports). Some organizations produce their own research journals, but many reports of government-supported research appear in periodicals and conference proceedings from non-official publishers. These can be identified if the sponsoring organization's publications list includes articles and papers written by its staff. Some officially-supported research is published commercially in book form and is available through the normal book-trade channels, including publications arising from ESRC sponsored projects like *Water demand forecasting* (Geo Books, 1986).

Until 1981 government reports were collected and made available by the Technology Report Centre, which also produced an abstracting service. Now the major source for British government research reports is the British Library Document Supply Centre. It includes them (without abstracts) in its monthly *British reports, translations and theses* and makes the reports available for loan.

Building Research Establishment

Two examples illustrate the work and publishing of government research organizations. The Building Research Establishment (BRE) is one of several carrying out research for government departments. It is concerned with all aspects of research into construction including housing defects, materials and services in buildings, and fire prevention. It organizes seminars to disseminate information from current research and offers an advisory service on construction problems. BRE issues all of its publications directly, many of them in series. The *BRE digests* are well-known concise summaries for building professionals, while the *Defect action sheets* help them to avoid common building faults in houses. The *Information papers* (up to 24 a year) are four-page summaries of recent BRE research and advice like *Defects in local authority housing* (IP 15/90). A new series of *Good building guides* (up to 12 a year) began in 1990. These concise publications provide advice like *Choosing between cavity, internal and external wall insulation* (GBG 5, 1990). More substantial reports and books appear in the *BRE report* series and include the standard guide on *Design of normal concrete mixes* (rev. ed., 1988) and a study of *The building Magnesian limestones of the British Isles* (1988). The BRE also produces films, videos and software packages to publicize its work and to train workers in the construction industry. BRE publications are fairly easy to trace. *BRE news of construction research* (six a year) contains details of recent publications and those currently available appear in a series of lists of *BRE publications* on topics like cement and concrete or non-traditional housing. BRE also produces the BRIX database (available on ESA-IRS) which covers literature on all aspects of building research, including BRE's own publications.[13]

Natural Environment Research Council

The Natural Environment Research Council (NERC) encourages research into the physical properties and biological aspects of the earth, the seas and the atmosphere. It has done important work in relation to the 'greenhouse effect' as part of its environmental monitoring programme and discovered the 'ozone hole' in Antarctica. The Council had a budget of £135 million in 1990/91 and supports 11 research units. These include the British Antarctic Survey studying the Antarctic environment and the British Geological Survey which is responsible for the Geological Survey maps and memoirs. NERC also provides funds to universities and polytechnics for research grants and studentships. Publication is largely decentralized with each unit responsible for the publishing arrangements for its own material. NERC itself publishes an annual report, publicity literature and two periodicals: *NERC news* (quarterly) and *The Researcher*. It also produces some reports like *Frontiers of earth sciences to the year 2000* (1989) which identifies future research priorities. Many of the British Geological Survey's publications are issued by HMSO while the Ordnance Survey publishes the Geological Survey maps on its behalf. Its extensive *Mineral reconnaissance programme report* series is published directly. HMSO also took over publication of the Institute of Terrestrial Ecology's books in 1988. The Deacon Laboratory of the Institute of Oceanographic Sciences publishes an extensive research report series. Most of the material put out by the Sea Mammal Research Unit appears in scientific periodicals, while the British Antarctic Survey publishes its own quarterly journal, *Antarctic science*. Publications lists must be sought from each of the institutes and units, not all of which produce one, or from the Ordnance Survey or HMSO.

NATIONAL HEALTH SERVICE AUTHORITIES

The National Health Service (NHS) was set up in 1948 to coordinate hospital and health care services and to provide a comprehensive range of medical services. It is a central government responsibility exercised through the health ministers of each constituent country of the UK. The NHS is a major service employing nearly a million people. Administration of the NHS is through health authorities and boards. England has a two-tier system with 14 Regional Health Authorities (RHAs) and 190 District Health Authorities. The RHAs are responsible for regional planning and resource allocation and the provision of specialized services, while districts at present control all health services in their area. The reorganization of the NHS in 1990 has allowed some hospitals to become self-governing, which affects this pattern. Scotland, Wales and Northern Ireland all have single-tier health boards or authorities, with their own government departments responsible for strategic planning. Family Health Services Authorities in England and Wales supervise services provided locally by doctors, dentists, pharmacists and opticians. Community health councils in each district in England and Wales and local health councils in Scotland provide an opportunity for consumer pressure and local views to be represented. Health Service Commissioners deal with cases of maladministration and other complaints. Their annual reports and reports of investigations are House of Commons Papers. The Health Education Authority became part of the NHS in 1987 when it replaced the Health Education Council. Separate health education bodies exist in Wales, Scotland and Northern Ireland.

Publications are issued by each RHA and district: a total of over 230 different publishers within the NHS. In addition there are publications from individual hospitals, Community Health Councils and the Health Education Authority. A large volume of publications is produced but many are difficult to find out about, especially for those outside the health service. Certain kinds of publications can be expected, however. Each authority produces an annual report and financial statement (these may be separate publications). An annual District Plan will set the goals and programmes for the coming year. The RHA issues a composite Regional Plan, a digest of which may be produced for a wider public. Consultation documents are important, like *Building a healthy Birmingham* (West Midlands RHA, 1989) which set out a radical reorganization of hospital provision there. Consultative publications are also issued on specific aspects of service, e.g. *Adult mental health − a strategy consultation document* (Clwyd Health Authority, 1986) or on a particular hospital or area. Statistics on a wide range of topics are needed for management information and some are also published, including statistics of in-patients and out-patients, waiting lists and abortion figures. Surveys are carried out to assess needs and current provision, like the *X-ray workload analysis* (Gwynedd Health Authority, 1986). Many health authorities issue statements of policy or guidelines on a variety of matters like administration of drugs, mental health services, and first aid. Individual services and hospital provision are reviewed in reports which may recommend improvements and changes to services, like *A report on the specialist health visiting service to travelling families* (City and Hackney Health Authority, 1988). Newspapers for NHS staff like *West Midlands health beat* (West Midlands RHA, six a year) keep them in touch with developments in each district. Health education and information material may be provided locally as well as by the Health Education Authority:

South Birmingham HA produces *Feet over 50* while West Birmingham HA issued a useful handbook for the disabled with details of services, facilities and benefits available. North West Thames RHA is one of the partners in *NHS direct*, a medical information service by telephone giving pre-recorded details of over 200 medical topics from hayfever to schizophrenia. Occasional historical publications may appear to mark a centenary or other anniversary, like the detailed study of *The Royal Berkshire Hospital 1839–1989* published by the hospital in 1989. Finally the library services in regions and districts issue bibliographies, periodicals lists, current awareness bulletins and occasionally lists of local health service publications.

This wealth of published material is rarely coordinated to any extent. Few health authorities have successfully implemented a publications policy, though use of ISBNs is becoming more common and production standards are rising. Roy Tabor includes recommendations for 'A publications policy for NHS authorities' as an appendix to his useful brief review of NHS publishing.[14] Publications may be free within the region but there is a growing tendency to charge other users. Bibliographic control depends substantially on the efforts of regional and district librarians to find out about and acquire publications. Some RHAs, including the West Midlands, issue lists of publications within their area. Some NHS publications are sent to the Department of Health Library and appear in its bibliographies and in the DHSS-DATA database. As with local authority publications, it is often difficult to trace what has been published by a particular authority, despite the potential value of such material to other health authorities and to students and researchers.

One group of NHS publications are easily obtained, however: those of the Health Education Authority (HEA).[15] It is the health promotion body for England but is responsible for public education on AIDS throughout Britain. In England it advises the government on health education matters and publishes health education materials. It also organizes advertising campaigns on television and in newspapers and periodicals. Its publications fall into three main groups: mainly free material for the general public distributed through local health promotion units; resource packs for schools available from commercial publishers; and publications for professionals like *Food for the heart: workplace campaign manual* (1990) and the HEA Research Report series. Publications include many posters and leaflets on alcohol, baby and childcare, dental health, food hygiene and sexually transmitted diseases. Some are in several languages: *Your right to health* is a 24-page booklet available in 12 different language versions. Most of the more substantial publications issued by the former Health Education Council have been discontinued, but the *Pregnancy book* (1984) is still available. Two periodicals are issued for health professionals: *Health education news* (bi-monthly) in tabloid newspaper format and the quarterly *Health education journal* which disseminates research and reviews books and audiovisual publications. A publications catalogue is available.

TRIBUNALS

A large number of administrative tribunals have been established in Britain to provide an accessible and relatively cheap way of resolving disputes. They may be called panels, boards, commissions or tribunals but all are quasi-judicial bodies. They have some of the functions of normal courts of law like the magistrates courts or Crown Courts, but hear many more cases. Each tribunal deals with one kind of dispute: there are social security appeal tribunals, industrial tribunals, tax tribunals, a data protection tribunal and many others. The dispute may be between private citizens and government departments over matters like social security benefits, or a claim by government bodies against individual citizens (tax tribunals), or disputes between citizens (industrial tribunals). It may involve a decision on rights, such as the right to enter the United Kingdom (Immigration Appeals Tribunal).

Tribunals are established by Act of Parliament and members are normally appointed by the appropriate government minister. Most have a legally qualified chairman and other members may have expert knowledge of the subject concerned. The composition and procedure of tribunals varies and they are not bound by precedent, so current decisions are not necessarily consistent with those in previous cases. Many tribunals have a right of appeal, and appeals on points of law may be made to the regular civil courts. There are over 60 separate tribunal systems in this country. Some are single tribunals while others consist of several courts in different parts of the country because of the large number of cases, like the Social Security Appeal Tribunals. Their work is reviewed by the Council on Tribunals which reports to Parliament.

The Industrial Tribunals are one of the best-known tribunal systems. They provide a way of settling disputes between employer and employee. Their work grew enormously in the 1970s as they became, in effect, a national system of labour courts dealing with employment legislation. They are concerned with unfair dismissal, redundancy, trade union membership rights, and discrimination on grounds of race or sex. There are 24 industrial tribunals throughout the country which make decisions on around 30,000 cases a year. Members include an employers' and a trade union representative nominated by the Department of Employment, with a legally qualified chairman. Many disputes are settled before reaching a tribunal. A conciliation officer of the Advisory, Conciliation and Arbitration Service (ACAS) receives the details of most cases and tries to mediate: ACAS handled nearly 50,000 cases involving individual conciliation in 1989. Only then does the case come before an Industrial Tribunal. Appeals against the tribunal's decisions on points of law go the Employment Appeal Tribunal.

Publications consist mainly of the reports of decisions in individual cases and booklets explaining the functions and procedure of the tribunal. Tribunals are not required to issue reports of cases, even though a number of them do. Reports of several tribunals are published by HMSO: Value Added Tax Tribunals, Immigration Appeals Tribunal and Social Security Commissioners' decisions are published in this way, though not all cases are reported. Some tribunals publish their own reports directly though these may be difficult to obtain: Transport Tribunal appeals appear in this way. Commercial publishers report decisions of certain tribunals: *Industrial case reports* (1976-) includes Employment Appeal Tribunal cases. The LEXIS online legal information system includes reports of cases from several tribunals. Not all tribunals publish their decisions and it may be difficult to obtain this information. Industrial Tribunals' decisions may be consulted at the Central Office of the Industrial Tribunals and at the appropriate Regional Office; individual cases are also often reported in the local press. Guides to the role and procedure of several tribunals are published either as free publications, like *Industrial Tribunals procedure*, or as HMSO publications e.g. *Medical Appeal Tribunals: a guide to procedure* (1987). Despite the fact that individuals are far more likely to appear before a tribunal than an ordinary court of law, the work of most tribunals remains little known.

References and further reading

1 Office of the Minister for the Civil Service, *Public bodies*, HMSO, annual.
2 Holland, P., *The Quango death list*, Adam Smith Institute, 1980.
3 Prime Minister's Office, *Report on non-departmental public bodies*, Cmnd.7797, HMSO, 1980.
4 The publishing of one privatized body is discussed in: Alsmeyer, D., 'British Telecom publications' in *Who publishes official*

information for business and industry? edited by Valerie J. Nurcombe, Library Association, Information Services Group, SCOOP, 1989, 69−74.

5   Bell, T. I. 'The Bank of England as a publisher' in *Who publishes official information for business and industry?* edited by Valerie J. Nurcombe, Library Association, Information Services Group, SCOOP, 1989, 51−6.

6   Toase, C. 'Reference books you may have missed', *Refer*, 5 (2), Autumn 1988, 14.

7   Pantry, S. 'Health and Safety Executive and Commission: publications and services' in *Who publishes official information on health, safety and social services?* edited by Valerie J. Nurcombe, Library Association, Information Services Group, SCOOP, 1989, 33−47.

8   Heynat, J., 'London Docklands Development Corporation' in *Who publishes official information for business and industry?* edited by Valerie J. Nurcombe, Library Association, Information Services Group, SCOOP, 1989, 75−9.

9   The work of the Highlands and Islands Development Board and the Scottish Development Agency is discussed in: Kirk, D., 'The changing rural economy: business information support', *Refer*, 6 (2), Summer 1990, 11−14.

10 McKinney, L., 'National Economic Development Office' in *Who publishes official information for business and industry?* edited by Valerie J. Nurcombe, Library Association, Information Services Group, SCOOP, 1989, 60−5.

11 Bassett, D., 'Museums and museum publications in Britain, 1975−85', *British book news*, May 1986, 263−73. (Although subtitled Part 1, a second part has not been published).

12 Wade, J., 'Publications of the Medical Research Council' in *Who publishes information on health, safety and social services?* edited by Valerie J. Nurcombe, Library Association, Information Services Group, SCOOP, 1989, 26−32.

13 Raisin, A., 'BRIX and ICONDA' in *British official publications online* edited by Valerie J. Nurcombe, Library Association, Information Services Group, SCOOP, 1990, 30−8.

14 Tabor, R., 'Publishing in the National Health Service − a view from the Wessex Regional Health Authority' in *Who publishes official information on health, safety and social services?* edited by Valerie J. Nurcombe, Library Association, Information Services Group, SCOOP, 1989, 53−7.

15 Martin, F., 'Health Education Authority publications: what is the Health Education Authority?' in *Who publishes official information on health, safety and social services?* edited by Valerie J. Nurcombe, Library Association, Information Services Group, SCOOP, 1989, 63 – 5.

5   *Bibliographic control and selection sources*

Adequate bibliographic control is important for all users of official publications to enable them to trace a specific title whether it was published within the last few months or 20 years ago, or to identify official material on a topic of interest. A complete record of the current output of official publications is desirable, no matter how or by whom they have been published. Librarians and booksellers in particular find it useful to have records of all the official publications currently available from their publishers, regardless of when they were originally published. Retrospective lists of official publications are helpful to researchers, historians and others who need older official publications which may now be available only in libraries. Many users are more concerned with finding what has been or is being published on any given topic than with identifying specific documents, and they need bibliographies with good subject access. The introduction of online and CD-ROM databases for official publications makes it easier for these requirements to be met by a single source.

OFFICIAL DATABASES

UKOP
The most complete single listing of all British official publications appears as a database issued jointly by HMSO and Chadwyck-Healey on a CD-ROM disc.[1] *UKOP, The Catalogue of United Kingdom official publications on CD-ROM* covers all HMSO publications, including international organizations' publications distributed by HMSO, and all non-HMSO publications from the official organizations recorded in the *Catalogue of British official publications* (q.v.). UKOP includes all publications from these sources since 1980, whether or not the item is still in print. The first CD-ROM disc appeared in 1989 with almost 160,000 records. It is updated quarterly with a cumulating disc containing

the complete file which appears within four weeks of the end of the quarter. It is still necessary to use current printed lists to find out about the most recent publications however. Prices and availability information are updated so that all in-print material can be traced. This is particularly useful for ascertaining whether copies of non-HMSO publications can be obtained from their original publishers.

UKOP costs £800 (+ VAT) a year which limits its sales potential, though public libraries receive a 50% discount. It is a powerful searching tool which is greatly superior to the printed sources. It overcomes the artificial distinction between HMSO and non-HMSO publications affecting other lists, which is especially helpful for organizations publishing both through HMSO and directly. It offers speed and convenience in searching and has a number of special features. The whole file may be searched, or HMSO or non-HMSO files individually, or particular kinds of publications, e.g. statutory instruments, parliamentary publications. Searches can be restricted to in-print publications only and current awareness searches for material added within the last quarter can be undertaken. Corporate authors, personal authors and chairmen, publishing bodies, keywords and series titles can all be checked in indexes before search terms are entered. This is particularly useful with corporate authors which are linked hierarchically as well as being listed alphabetically: entering the name of a parent organization like a government department retrieves a list of its sub-bodies as well. For sub-bodies the name of the parent organization is given. References are provided from acronyms and previous names. HMSO and Chadwyck-Healey have cross-referenced variants in their usage of corporate author names between the databases. This helps users to understand the relationships between official bodies and facilitates searching.

UKOP offers the user menu choices to select, with windows to display more detailed information. When examining brief citations, one item can be selected and a window opened giving the full citation, for instance. A limitation is that the workspace on screen holds a maximum of 12 lines so that space must be cleared quite frequently; the deleted searches or references cannot be recalled. Searches can be carried out using a variety of approaches: by corporate body, personal author, chairman, series title, keyword or subject, publisher, year of publication, parliamentary session, price, and ISBN or ISSN. These can be combined to retrieve a statutory instrument issued in 1988 on data protection or a Home Office publication on a fire incident in 1985. Publications can often be identified even when the user has provided incomplete or only partially correct details. Subject searches are limited to the words of titles and series titles and the few subject terms selected for the indexes of the printed equivalents of the files. There is a choice of formats when downloading or printing out items from the database. Data can be downloaded in MARC format for automated library catalogues or printed out as catalogue cards; order forms can be generated and records can be printed out in full or with just the essential bibliographic information. The coverage and the searching facilities make UKOP the easiest and most convenient source to consult for official publications since 1980. Only the most recent publications must be looked for elsewhere.

HMSO database

The HMSO publications listed in UKOP can also be traced in an online database: the HMSO file on BLAISE-LINE and the *British official publications (HMSO)* file on DIALOG. HMSO has maintained its own computer file of its publications since 1976. It offers instant updating for new titles, rather than the monthly updating of the HMSO public database. It has been available in HMSO bookshops and for use by some government departments for several years, but the long-promised public database became available in 1989. This covers all HMSO publications (parliamentary, non-parliamentary and Northern Ireland titles) and all agency publications from British official bodies and international organizations sold by HMSO.

The HMSO database in both online and CD-ROM forms offers new searching facilities for tracing government publications. In particular, the ISBN prefix can be used to limit the search to a specific type of publication or government body. 0101 can be used when only a Command Paper is required, while 01134 will produce Home Office publications. Combined with subject words this is a useful searching aid. Parliamentary publications and statutory instruments can also be searched by session or year and number, which is helpful if the enquirer knows the specific number and date. Many other fields can be searched, including title, personal author or chairman, and date limitations can be applied. However, the nature of the HMSO record restricts searching: subject headings are merely the strings of terms chosen as index entries and subject searching still depends on these or the other words of the title. No class mark or abstract is included within the record. Another irritant to most searchers is the inclusion of separate records for each issue of a serial, following HMSO catalogue practice.

BLAISE-LINE search software introduces its own restrictions as proximity indicators, which allow the user to specify that words must be adjacent, cannot be used. When searching for material on the British Council, for instance, even restricting the search to the publisher field produces many irrelevant entries. This is not a problem with the more powerful DIALOG search software which allows several degrees of proximity to be specified. The cost of searching the two files is about equal.

The HMSO online file is updated monthly and is therefore significantly more current than UKOP. Even so, unlike HMSO's internal database, it is not completely up-to-date and other HMSO sources must be checked for the most recent titles. The HMSO database has a longer backfile (1976 to date) than UKOP, which may give it the edge for some retrospective searches. Both UKOP and the HMSO online database have the same amount of information in each record and share similar limitations in subject searching. They offer the greater convenience of searching the whole file in one action rather than the consultation of many annual cumulations and updating issues required with the printed sources. The online and CD-ROM files both have many more access points than the printed bibliographies, and references do not have to be laboriously copied out. Like UKOP, the HMSO database can be used for cataloguing as well as bibliographic searches and catalogue data in MARC format can be downloaded for incorporation into a local catalogue.

Chadwyck-Healey made the *British official publications (non-HMSO)* online file available on DIALOG in 1987 but withdrew it at the end of 1989. This was partly a commercial decision to help sales of UKOP and partly because the revenue from online use did not cover the cost of making the database available. Its withdrawal is unfortunate for the many libraries which have access to DIALOG and could use this file, but which do not necessarily subscribe to UKOP.

PRINTED BIBLIOGRAPHIES: HMSO PUBLICATIONS

HMSO has a long-established series of lists and catalogues which record publications recently issued and indicate which titles are still in print. Because these lists and catalogues have been published for many years they also form a retrospective record of British government publications for the major part of this century. This printed record has been partially superseded by the HMSO online database and UKOP on CD-ROM for users with access to these sources. There are weaknesses in HMSO's recording of its publications, but they are better controlled bibliographically than the non-HMSO official publications. Users of

HMSO's lists and records must always be aware of why they are produced: they are primarily sales lists to help HMSO's staff, its agents and other booksellers to identify what has been published recently and which older titles can still be obtained. The bibliographical details given are usually the minimum required for identification and there are few annotations to describe the publications. Access by subject is relatively weak because it is of less relevance to HMSO and its booksellers, though HMSO has recognized the need to provide lists on individual subjects and for particular types of user. The printed lists and catalogues are compiled from HMSO's internal database, to which records of new publications are added daily.

Table 5   Summary of main current listings of HMSO publications

1. **HMSO Database**
   Covers all HMSO's own publications and agency titles from 1976 with monthly updates. Available on BLAISE-LINE and DIALOG.

2. **UKOP: Catalogue of United Kingdom Official Publications**
   A CD-ROM disc combining all HMSO and non-HMSO official publications since 1980, with quarterly updates.

3. **HMSO in Print**
   Microfiche listing of in-print material only, with quarterly updates. Includes statutory instruments.

4. **HMSO Daily List**
   Essential as none of the above provide up to the minute listings. Everything published on the day: parliamentary, non-parliamentary, statutory instruments, agency publications. Also on Prestel for one week.

5. **HMSO Monthly Catalogue**
   Cumulation of recent parliamentary, non-parliamentary and agency publications (statutory instruments not included). Cumulating index throughout the year.

6. **HMSO Annual Catalogue**
   HMSO's own publications only, excluding statutory instruments. Arrangement, headings and indexing not consistent from year to year. Separate *HMSO Agency catalogue* for publications of international and British bodies sold by HMSO.

7. **Subject Catalogues**
   Selective listings of in-print material for publicity. Re-issued every
   one to two years. Often annotated.

8. **Sectional Lists**
   A series listing mainly non-parliamentary in-print publications by
   department. Few now updated frequently.

9. **British National Bibliography/BNB-MARC File**
   Higher standard of entry information and indexing. Useful if exclusions
   taken into account. Slow at listing new titles.

10. **List of Statutory Instruments**
    Monthly, with annual cumulation. Useful if searching specifically
    for SIs by number or subject.

Daily lists

HMSO is very unusual among publishers in needing a daily list to keep
track of its output. The *Daily list* appears five times a week and lists
between 30 and 50 titles in each issue, most of which are published that
day. It includes HMSO's own parliamentary and non-parliamentary
publications, publications sold by HMSO on behalf of other British
official bodies and international organizations (agency publications), and
the statutory instruments issued that day, each in a separate section. Basic
bibliographical details of each title are given but the list is unannotated.
Libraries receive the *Daily list* by post, either in daily or weekly batches,
which involves some delay in identifying the most recent publications.
The most up-to-date information on what HMSO has published appears
daily on Prestel, British Telecom's videotext information service. Titles
are displayed for one week after publication, but certain publications
like *Hansard* and the *Business monitors* are omitted. Information is also
given on forthcoming non-parliamentary publications, sectional lists and
subject catalogues available, and addresses of HMSO agents. *Daily lists*
remain of value to libraries using the HMSO online database since the
latter is only updated monthly.

Monthly catalogue and Annual catalogue

The *HMSO monthly catalogue* lists anew all the publications which have
appeared in the *Daily list* for the month with the exception of statutory
instruments which have their own separate *List of statutory instruments*

(q.v.). The *Monthly catalogue* is arranged in four main parts: firstly, parliamentary publications by type of paper; then the 'classified section' which combines parliamentary and non-parliamentary publications in a single sequence alphabetically under the name of the body responsible for each. Northern Ireland publications and titles sold but not published by HMSO (mainly publications from international organizations) have separate sections. A fairly detailed alphabetical index, which very usefully cumulates throughout the year, provides name and subject access. It is produced automatically by the desktop publishing software. An ISBN index appeared in the monthly and annual catalogues for several years but was dropped in 1990. The *HMSO annual catalogue* is arranged in the same way as the *Monthly catalogue* except that publications sold by HMSO on behalf of other organizations like the World Health Organization and the European Communities appear in a separate catalogue. Until 1985 this listed only the publications of international organizations, but from 1986 it became the *HMSO agency catalogue* with material from a few British official bodies as well.

These current catalogues are useful for identifying individual documents when the issuing body is known but are less reliable when approached by title or subject. Although the indexes are more detailed than those before 1976 they still have distinct limitations. They contain name entries for authors and editors of official publications and for chairmen of committees. Title entries under the first word of each title are not provided. Instead subject keywords and phrases are selected: *Private sector involvement in the remand system* appears not under 'Private' as it would in normal title indexing but under 'Remand system. Private sector involvement. Proposals'. In some cases publications are listed under two or three keywords. The effect is to create a subject index which provides some consistency through choice of entry term but which is ultimately dependent on the words used in the title.

Users may experience some difficulty even when searching under issuing body, particularly in retrospective searches, because of changes in heading or arrangement of the *Annual catalogue*. Prior to 1976 most publications were grouped under the main government department responsible. From 1976 the headings in the classified section were based on HMSO's version of the *Anglo-American cataloguing rules* (explained in the *Annual catalogue 1976*, pp.427 – 34). This led to scattering of related material: general publications on defence appeared under 'Ministry of Defence' but defence publications were also listed under Air Force Department, Army Department, etc. Cross-references were

131

provided in some annual catalogues but not in others. Modifications to headings since 1988 have reduced this scattering. The publications of committees, working parties, and advisory groups appear under the name of the committee. Numerically designated committees like the '4th Standing Committee on Statutory Instruments etc', are filed in numerical order before the beginning of the alphabetical sequence. The arrangement of the *Annual catalogue* is not necessarily consistent from year to year: in the 1986 and 1987 catalogues parliamentary and non-parliamentary publications are listed entirely separately instead of being combined in the classified section. Much care is needed in any retrospective search using these printed lists.

The HMSO catalogues have been criticized for the long delays in the appearance of cumulations. This creates extra work in bibliographical checking to trace a recent publication. Delays were particularly bad in 1986 and 1987 because of the loss of the database from which catalogues were produced. Speed of production of cumulations is currently satisfactory with the *HMSO annual catalogue* appearing within two months of the end of the year and the *Monthly catalogue* coming out within four to six weeks.

In-print listings

The printed lists and catalogues discussed so far enable users to trace current or older material published or sold by HMSO, but do not reveal whether they are still available. This can be found through *HMSO in print on microfiche*, which is updated quarterly and lists available HMSO publications, both parliamentary and non-parliamentary, including statutory instruments. Access is by title, number for parliamentary publications, department, and author or chairman. All the information in *HMSO in print* is available more easily from UKOP and the HMSO online database, so it is useful mainly for those libraries without the electronic sources.

Subscribers have much more up-to-date and more comprehensive information than is given by the declining series of *Sectional lists*. Twenty lists were still available in 1990 when the series was revised. New titles appeared which expanded coverage or included material from several previous lists, like SL 21 *Employment, health and safety*. Sectional lists give details of mainly current non-parliamentary publications from government departments (SL 3. *Energy, Trade and Industry*) or other bodies (SL 73. *Museums and galleries*). They are usually arranged by subject or series and most have no index. Government departments are reluctant to pay for revision of these free lists so not all are updated very frequently. *Sectional lists* are of some value to those without access to *HMSO in print*, UKOP or the HMSO online database, but many of the lists are two or more years out of date.

Subject catalogues

HMSO publications are relatively easy to trace if the organization responsible is known, but it can be more difficult to find out what has been published on a particular subject. Several government bodies may issue publications on different aspects of a topic: the Home Office produced a report on *Schools, disruptive behaviour and delinquency* (1988) while the OPCS surveyed *Smoking among secondary school children in 1986* (1987) and the DES issued guidance on *Crime prevention in schools* (1987). The *Sectional lists* are only partially helpful and it is easy to miss publications in the *Annual catalogue* and *Monthly catalogue* if the searcher has not anticipated the terms used in the title. Only by using the HMSO database or UKOP would a search under the term 'school(s)' bring these titles together. HMSO provides some selective subject lists for publications currently in print, both HMSO's own and some from international organizations like the European Communities and the United Nations. Over 20 lists exist, many updated regularly and often with useful descriptions of content and level. Topics covered include agriculture, forestry and fisheries, art, education, science and technology and history. Some are short lists featuring a handful of titles, while others are extensive catalogues arranged by subject and with title indexes like the useful *Social issues catalogue* introduced in 1988. These catalogues appeal to people interested in the subject as well as to booksellers and librarians.

Forthcoming publications

The lists and catalogues dealt with so far record publications once they have been published, but HMSO also produces lists of forthcoming titles. A selective seasonal catalogue of forthcoming titles likely to be of interest to booksellers is published. HMSO also issues prospectuses for individual publications and series describing them and sometimes including sample pages. It is impossible to provide an exact list of forthcoming parliamentary publications as many are published at short notice. Details of some selected forthcoming non-parliamentary titles appear in HMSO's Prestel frames. The weekly *At press* is a useful advance guide to new titles, new editions and reprints sent for printing during the week, though there are no descriptions of books included. These will be published several weeks later, or even several months for hardback books.

Other HMSO lists and indexes

A selective listing for distribution to local authorities is produced: the *Weekly list: a selection of interest to local authorities*. This groups official publications, including those from international organizations, under broad subject headings reflecting local government responsibilities. It is designed only to draw attention to the existence of new publications: they are not described. HMSO produces the quarterly *Committee reports published by HMSO indexed by chairman* which lists reports published during the period under the name of the chairman of the committee or working party. The fourth issue each year is the annual cumulation. *New books HMSO* is a useful selective list of about 40 titles with annotations which is issued irregularly, usually covering two or three months. It draws attention to some of the major, mainly non-parliamentary, publications issued.

BNB, POLIS and the Checklist

Some bibliographies not published by HMSO include large quantities of HMSO publications and may be superior in indexing and arrangement. They can be used safely for bibliographical checking if their coverage and limitations are understood. The *British national bibliography* (weekly) has listed HMSO publications since 1950 with a clearly defined coverage which is explained in the introduction to each cumulative volume. It excludes certain categories of HMSO publications such as bills, routine House of Commons papers, statutory instruments and circulars, but provides good coverage of most non-parliamentary publications, acts and Command Papers. The user of BNB can be confident of having proper title indexing under first word of title, a systematic subject arrangement which brings together HMSO publications and books from other publishers on the same topic, and a good standard of subject indexing. The subject approach to official publications is much more safely pursued in BNB, within its limitations, than in the HMSO lists and catalogues, or even in the HMSO database or UKOP. The same data are also included in the BNB-MARC files on BLAISE-LINE which offer a considerable range of search options. Unfortunately BNB is slow in listing new HMSO publications. A further limitation is the omission of international organizations publications found in the HMSO lists because they do not have a British imprint.

The POLIS database (q.v.) includes bibliographic information on parliamentary and non-parliamentary publications since the beginning of the 1980s. It is a convenient search tool for its small group of users. The British Library puts out an irregular *Checklist of British official serial publications* (12th ed., 1987) to identify serials currently available from official bodies. About 13% of the entries are for periodicals, yearbooks and series currently published by HMSO. It is a good way of checking for serial publications, though individual publications within series are not separately listed.

Retrospective searching

HMSO publications may retain their value for many years after their first appearance. Documents like the Beveridge Report *Social insurance and allied services* Cmd. 6404 (HMSO, 1942) are still referred to. Other older publications may no longer have any current relevance but acquire historical significance as contributions to their subject. Many of the 19th-century reports like that of the Royal Commission on Trade Unions, 1868, have become mines of information — social, economic and cultural as well as political — for the historian. As with current searching, users want to identify what has been published on a subject as well as trace specific documents.

Retrospective searching for HMSO publications is possible through the HMSO database, UKOP and the index to the *Annual catalogue* for recent years. The *Consolidated index to government publication* has covered five-year periods from 1936−40 to 1976−80. Continuous pagination was used in the *Annual catalogue* throughout each five-year period to make index references unambiguous. A drawback is that the *Annual catalogue* index and the *Consolidated index* were prepared by different contractors and entry terms are not always consistent. A commercial publication which provides a more convenient way of checking for HMSO publications issued during a 50-year period is the *Cumulative index to the annual catalogues of Her Majesty's Stationery Office publications, 1922−1972* (2 vols, Carrollton Press, 1976). The entries for all HMSO publications are here in a single alphabetical sequence. The indexing is of the same standard as that in the *Annual catalogues*: it has been cumulated but not systematically overhauled and improved. It is more convenient than *Catalogues and indexes of British government publications 1920−1970* (5 vols, 1974) from Chadwyck-Healey, which reprints the consolidated indexes but does not cumulate them. Earlier HMSO material can be found in *The sale catalogues of*

British government publications 1836–1921 (four vols, 1977) from Oceana.

Anyone carrying out a retrospective search must be aware of the considerable difference in indexing and arrangement of the *Annual catalogue* prior to 1976 since there is no online version for this period. Entries were then grouped mainly under the headings for the government department responsible and not the individual bodies or committees issuing publications. The publications of the Countryside Commission, the Building Research Establishment and the Ancient Monuments Board, for instance, all appeared under 'Environment, Department of the'. Indexing was also less exhaustive with fewer subject terms for each document.

There are better bibliographical sources for retrospective subject searching, though the tools discussed above are suitable for identifying specific documents. BNB and BNB-MARC can be searched back to 1950 by subject or issuing body and title. The British Library *General catalogue of printed books* is of some use for identifying older government publications which are grouped under the heading 'England' and then by department or agency. An *England sub-headings index* volume help-fully locates publications by issuing body. The British Library catalogue is also searchable as the BLC file on BLAISE-LINE or as a set of CD-ROM discs. These provide more access points than the printed catalogue.

For most users the best aids to identifying many older HMSO publications are the select lists and breviates compiled by Percy and Grace Ford and Diana Marshallsay:

Ford, Percy and Grace, *Select list of British parliamentary papers, 1833–1899*, Blackwell, 1953.

Ford, Percy and Grace, *A breviate of parliamentary papers, 1900–1916*, Blackwell, 1957.

Ford, Percy and Grace, *A breviate of parliamentary papers, 1917–1939*, Blackwell, 1951.

Ford, Percy and Grace, *A breviate of parliamentary papers, 1940–1954*, Blackwell, 1961.

Ford, Percy and others, *Select list of British parliamentary papers, 1955–1964*, Irish University Press, 1970.

Marshallsay, D. and Smith, J. H., *Ford list of British parliamentary papers, 1965–1974*, KTO Press, 1979.

Marshallsay, D and Richards, P. G., *Ford list of British parliamentary papers, 1974–1983*, Chadwyck-Healey, 1989.

Despite the apparent restriction to parliamentary publications, selected non-parliamentary publications are included, especially after 1922 when the Treasury instructed government departments to reduce the number of parliamentary publications. More routine material like administrative reports and statistical returns are excluded together with publications on foreign relations, military and naval matters. The select lists give only the bibliographical details needed to trace each paper, including reference to the appropriate sessional volume for parliamentary papers. The breviates contain substantial summaries of each document: that for the Beveridge Report takes five pages, for instance. All volumes are arranged under broad subjects like 'Trade and industry' or 'Health', each of which is subdivided. There is a brief subject index and an index to chairmen in each volume. They are useful guides to the researcher requiring official publications on a broad range of economic, social, industrial, legal and administrative matters.

Separate breviates of parliamentary papers have been published for Northern Ireland since 1922 and for Ireland as a whole in the 19th century:

Maltby, A. and J., *Ireland in the nineteenth century: a breviate of official publications*, Pergamon Press, 1979.

Maltby, A., *The government of Northern Ireland 1922–72: a catalogue and breviate of parliamentary papers*, Irish University Press, 1974.

Indexes to chairmen

Most government reports, whether from parliamentary Select Committees, departmental committees, working parties or advisory bodies, are commonly referred to by the name of their chairmen: the Butler-Sloss report on child abuse; the McDonald report of the 'Beat the Cowboys' working party; or the very appropriate Diamond report on wealth. The indexes to HMSO catalogues include the names of chairmen but the quarterly *Committee reports published by HMSO indexed by chairman* and its annual cumulations are the most convenient way of tracing recent reports in this way. For retrospective searching a series of lists published by the Library Association identify reports from 1800 onwards under the names of chairmen:

Richard, Stephen, *British government publications: an index to chairmen and authors*, Vol 1: 1800–1899; vol 2: 1900–1940; vol 3: 1941–1978; vol 4: 1979–1982, Library Association, 1974–84.[2]

These provide speedy identification for the great majority of reports published by HMSO, though the first three volumes exclude most non-HMSO official reports. They help to reduce the confusion caused by the same chairman being responsible for several reports on different topics. Lord Scarman has been responsible for more than 50 reports on topics like family law and liability for defective products. Most users know only of *the* Scarman report for the topic in which they are interested and are unaware of the ambiguity of their request.

Clearly, the bibliographic control of HMSO publications is quite comprehensive in terms of listing current publications, recording what is in print, and being able to trace older publications. The main weakness lies in the subject approach where the HMSO database, UKOP, and non-official lists and bibliographies should be used to compensate for the lack of a subject arrangement and inadequate indexing in the printed sources.

BIBLIOGRAPHIC CONTROL OF NON-HMSO PUBLICATIONS

The bibliographic control of publications issued directly by government departments and other official bodies has developed much more recently than for HMSO publications. It is strongest in listing current publications, but even here is far from complete. It is easier to trace specific documents or publications from individual organizations than to pursue material on a subject. Retrospective coverage before 1980 other than through bibliographies from a few individual organizations, is virtually non-existent. This section concentrates mainly on the current listings of new and recent non-HMSO publications.

Table 6   Summary of main current listings for non-HMSO publications

---

1. **UKOP: Catalogue of United Kingdom Official Publications**
   CD-ROM disc combining all HMSO and non-HMSO publications since 1980 with quarterly updates. Non-HMSO material is from CoBOP.

2. **Catalogue of British Official Publications**
   Major printed listing of non-HMSO publications since 1980. Six issues a year plus annual cumulation. Covers all government departments and many other official bodies. Subject index. Separate cumulating *Keyword index* on microfiche.

3. **Checklist of British Official Serial Publications**
   Alphabetical list of official serials from the British Library indicating publisher and availability. Irregular updates.

4. **British National Bibliography/BNB-MARC File**
   Much less useful than for HMSO publications. Lists some material not in CoBOP.

5. **British Report, Translations and Theses/SIGLE File**
   Monthly listing from Document Supply Centre. Includes government (and local government) report literature. Broad subject headings. Keyword indexing.

6. **Directory of British Official Publications**
   Indicates kinds of publications produced by over 1,300 bodies and whether they issue a publications list. Needs updating.

7. **Publications Lists from Individual Bodies**
   These lists and catalogues vary greatly in completeness, informativeness and indexing. Most do not include forthcoming titles. Not available from all bodies.

8. **Databases**
   Publications of some official bodies are included in bibliographic databases e.g. HSELINE, DHSS-DATA.

Catalogue of British official publications

A great step forward in bibliographic control of non-HMSO publications occurred in 1981 with the appearance of the *Catalogue of British official publications not published by HMSO* (CoBOP).[3] Until this date a bibliographical search for a non-HMSO official publication involved checking whether the organization's publications were covered in any general or subject bibliography, and if not, whether the organization produced its own list of publications in some form. If the issuing organization was not known or the user was looking for official material on a subject the chances of finding anything were slim. CoBOP brought together for the first time the publications of over 300 official bodies in a single bibliography. It is published by Chadwyck-Healey, specialists in microform publishing. CoBOP covers non-HMSO publications since 1980 with bi-monthly issues and annual cumulations. Its coverage has grown from 3,500 publications in the 1980 annual volume to over 11,700 individual publications and 454 current periodical titles from over 500 official organizations in 1989.

CoBOP does not set out to cover all the types of official bodies dealt with in this book. Publications from only 45% of the organizations listed in the *Directory of British official publications* (2nd ed., 1984) were covered by CoBOP.[4] It includes publications from every government department: these comprise over 60% of the entries when associated bodies like Cadw and ADAS, whose publications are listed under the heading for the parent department, are taken into account. Among the non-departmental official bodies CoBOP is particularly strong in its coverage of research organizations, advisory bodies and some types of executive bodies. There are certain deliberate exclusions: maps from the Ordnance Survey or patents from the Patent Office which have their own efficient listings, for instance. Some organizations are omitted because they are unwilling to cooperate in giving details of their publications. Other omissions are evident: the Post Office Users' National Council is in, but material from the Post Office itself is not listed. Although some arts bodies like the Arts Council of Great Britain (covered since 1983) and the arts councils for Scotland, Wales and Northern Ireland (since 1987) became contributors, there is no coverage of most national libraries, museums and galleries as they are regarded as outside the scope of CoBOP.[3] A number of the regional electricity boards submitted details of their publications, but not the regional arts associations (now boards) or regional health authorities. Even when bodies are included there is no guarantee that the list of their publications will be complete. IWAAC, like most advisory bodies, publishes relatively little, but only three of the eight titles it produced between 1980 and 1989 are in CoBOP. None of the National Consumer Council Policy Papers, 35 of which were issued in 1987 alone, are listed. These may be excluded because they are not regarded as true publications: internal reports and house journals intended only for staff are omitted. CoBOP is the best single source for tracing non-HMSO official publications but it should not be assumed to be comprehensive.

Compilation of CoBOP depends on the voluntary submission of information about publications by the organization concerned. Most kinds of publications are included, from single page notices and letters to substantial books and reports. Periodicals and some audiovisual materials, maps and posters are also listed. Material is excluded if it is too ephemeral and its information has only very short-term value. Coverage of circulars and notices from government departments is variable, probably because

140

some departments may not consider them to be publications or the editor regards their information as ephemeral. Press releases were omitted when CoBOP first started but are now listed as they often contain information not available elsewhere. They form a substantial part of the output of some bodies: about 30% of all entries in the 1988 CoBOP were in this category. The individual listing of research reports and other material issued in series is particularly useful.

CoBOP lists publications alphabetically by the name of the issuing body, with government departments under the subject word of their title, i.e. Environment, Department of the. An index of contributing organizations in each issue shows what each has published. This is especially useful for locating organizations whose publications are listed under a parent body. Bibliographical details are basic but usually adequate. Many titles lack ISBNs but this is the responsibility of their publishers. The price of a publication or whether it is free is now indicated much more consistently than in early volumes of CoBOP. Many publications are available on microfiche from Chadwyck-Healey: this is clearly indicated by the microfiche reference number. There is also a number to identify the source from which publications can be obtained, keyed to an address list. This is extremely useful as one organization may have many different addresses for its publications. Periodicals appear as separate lists in the first and last issues of each year recording all titles available from the official bodies covered. New periodical titles during the year appear separately in other issues of CoBOP when they are first notified to the compilers.

There is a combined name and subject index: names are of personal authors of publications and of official bodies which do not appear as headings in the main entries sequence. The subject entries are fairly broad but are subdivided to reveal specific aspects clearly. The index entries for 'Agriculture − soil − moisture content' and 'Soil − moisture content − measurement' both lead to *Soil moisture measurement by microwave attenuation* (AFRC Institute of Engineering Research, 1987), for instance. The index does not include title entries as such, nor is it possible to find a publication under all keywords of its title. This can only be done by subscribing to the separate *Keyword index to British official publications* on microfiche (Chadwyck-Healey, bi-monthly). It is enhanced with many additional index terms and is updated cumulatively within the year so that only the latest index need be searched. Users of the printed CoBOP need the *Keyword index* quite frequently to trace known titles and to supplement CoBOP's subject indexing. Unlike the

Keyword index CoBOP's own index does not cumulate progressively during the year.

Despite some shortcomings CoBOP has established itself as an essential bibliographic tool which has listed 80,000 non-HMSO publications in its first decade. It is a convenient and easy to use source for a considerable proportion of non-HMSO official publications. The comments on coverage, exclusions and indexing apply as much to the non-HMSO section of UKOP as to the printed CoBOP. There are some differences between the two, however. UKOP offers greater flexibility in searching and much more convenient retrospective searches. It also records whether or not a title is still available from its original publisher. CoBOP is often more up to date than the quarterly UKOP because of its six issues a year.

British national bibliography

The *British national bibliography* and BNB-MARC database on BLAISE-LINE is much less satisfactory in its coverage of non-HMSO publications than of HMSO material. There is no clear statement of coverage and exclusions, though in practice many non-HMSO publications are omitted because they comprise kinds of material not listed by BNB. A major omission is 'promotional' material which is important to many official bodies wishing to make their work and services known to a wider public. Most leaflets and pamphlets of only a few pages are also omitted, which eliminates a substantial amount of non-HMSO material. Its exclusion of 'unpublished' material hits official documents intended primarily for internal circulation but also made available outside in limited numbers. Substantial reports like the Building Research Establishment's report series are listed individually, but briefer ones like the *BRE digests* are treated as serials. As with HMSO publications, routine administrative material like circulars, press releases and letters are omitted. A considerable proportion of the non-HMSO output therefore falls outside BNB's scope.

Although BNB has access to official publications received by the Legal Deposit Office its limited coverage of non-HMSO publications has been demonstrated by Johansson, Richard and Tolley.[5] Comparisons of titles in publications lists of official bodies with coverage by BNB showed significant differences in the extent of coverage. Thirty-three of the 72 Arts Council publications in its 1980/81 catalogue appeared in BNB. Far fewer Home Office publications were recorded: just 13 of the 238 titles in its 1980 publications list, though a significant proportion of its output was press releases and other categories omitted by BNB.[6]

Despite BNB's patchy coverage of non-HMSO publications it does record some titles not in CoBOP. This includes material from organizations not covered by CoBOP like English Heritage and the national museums and galleries. The two bibliographies may also differ in the range of titles listed from the same organization.[7] In some cases it is therefore worth checking both BNB and CoBOP for the publications of a particular organization. Where both bibliographies cover the same publication BNB usually takes significantly longer to list it. BNB seems best in its coverage of those public bodies which most closely resemble commercial publishers like the BBC, the British Museum and the Design Council. Finally, it is worth remembering two British Library files on BLAISE- LINE (HSS for humanities and social sciences material and SRIS for science and technology) for non-HMSO publications since 1975. These include some of the official publications received at the British Library under legal deposit but not listed in BNB.

Other major bibliographies

The *Checklist of British official serial publications* (12th ed., 1987) issued irregularly by the British Library is a useful aid to identifying official serials whether published by HMSO or directly. Its coverage is quite broad though it excludes material from the nationalized industries, public corporations, and museums and galleries as well as local and regional publications. Just under 2,000 serials of all types are included: periodicals, annual reports, occasional publications, report series, and monograph and pamphlet series. Two-thirds are current titles published directly by official organizations. The frequency, availability and issuing body is indicated for each title, and there is an index of issuing bodies. The *Checklist* is useful to confirm the existence and availability of a particular serial but it does not list individual issues.

British reports, translations and theses, a monthly current awareness service from the British Library Document Supply Centre, aims to list all grey literature received by the DSC. It specifically covers 'selected British official publications of a report nature that are not published by HMSO' from both central and local government. This includes many government report series such as those from the Royal Aerospace Establishment, Farnborough, and the Transport and Road Research Laboratory. Some are not strictly research reports: circulars from the Department of the Environment and publicity material from the National Health Service are listed, for instance.

Searching in the printed copies is hindered by the broad subject headings, especially in the social sciences and humanities. A keyword index in each monthly issue, with cumulations in microfiche, allows searching by one or more subject words from the title. The records are also available online as part of the SIGLE grey literature database available on BLAISE-LINE. For the user requiring report literature *British reports, translations and theses* can be a useful back-up to CoBOP.

Publications lists from individual organizations

Searches to identify non-HMSO publications are usually best started in CoBOP or UKOP unless the issuing body is known and its publications list is to hand. If the required organization or publication is not included in these bibliographies, more specific sources will need to be used. Whether an organization produces a publications list and in what form it appears can be confirmed in the *Directory of British official publications* (Mansell, 2nd ed., 1984). This is a listing of over 1,300 national and regional official bodies with information on the kinds of publications produced, the availability of publications lists and the address for information and orders. The 'Organizations index' should always be consulted because bodies subordinate to government departments are listed under the departmental entry in the main sequence. The directory is a valuable source in identifying official publishing organizations and a new edition is in preparation.

Some of the best lists of publications come from government department libraries and are bibliographies attempting to cover the department's total output. Some include both HMSO and non-HMSO publications while others list non-HMSO material only. The majority of these lists are annual and include only the publications of the year, like the *Home Office list of publications*. The interpretation of what constitutes a 'publication' differs somewhat from department to department, but some include audiovisual materials, circulars and press releases. A few of the lists record publications from bodies associated with the department: the Department of Trade and Industry's annual *Publications* list includes material from the Office of Fair Trading, Office of Telecommunications and even Department of Energy (which also issues its own separate list). This illustrates the value of checking the *Directory of British official publications* to locate a publications list. Some lists are unindexed (e.g. Home Office), some have title indexes only (Department of Trade and Industry), while a few have good subject indexes (Department of the Environment/Department of Transport).

Not all government departments produce full lists of their publications: the Department of Education and Science issues separate lists for *DES circulars and statistical bulletins*, and for publications from H.M. Inspectorate of Schools and its Architects and Building Branch. Others like the Treasury and the Ministry of Defence issue no separate list at all. Publications lists may change scope or be discontinued: the Department of the Environment/Department of Transport Library Services *Annual list of publications* used to include material from related bodies like its research establishments, but these are now excluded.

Publications lists from other public bodies vary greatly in quality and comprehensiveness. A number are as good as the best of the government department lists: the National Economic Development Office's annual catalogue and the Health and Safety Executive's *Publications in series*, for instance. Several bodies issue seasonal catalogues of new and forthcoming titles and stock lists of in-print publications comparable to those from commercial publishers. These include organizations with publishing subsidiaries like the British Museum Press and BBC Books as well as bodies like the Design Council, the Tate Gallery and the British Council. These catalogues are attractively designed, often with colour illustrations, and usually include synopses of most titles which can be helpful in selection.

Many official bodies make do with less informative lists. These may have few details beyond the title and price, like the *Arts Council publications* list which records 35 titles, some of them quite substantial publications, on a single sheet. This kind of list tells the user very little about the title they are seeking. It records what is available at a particular point in time, but will not necessarily be updated regularly to include new titles. However, such lists may provide access to details of publications not recorded in any other bibliographical source. Libraries have to make a special effort to obtain these lists, contacting each organization individually and sending periodic reminders if a new list has not been received. Publications lists are recorded in CoBOP for those bodies covered there.

A considerable number of official bodies issue no separate publications list at all: under half of the organizations in the *Directory of British official publications* have their output recorded in a publications list. If these bodies are poorly covered in the general bibliographies of official material then finding details of their publications may become very difficult. This is where more regular updating of the *Directory of British official publications* would be particularly valuable to establish whether a list in any form is available. In some cases the annual report of the organization may be the only source, as for the Royal Greenwich Observatory. Bibliographical details are likely to be minimal and the gap between the appearance of the publication and its listing in the annual report may be considerable. Some bodies have other regular publications which record their output like the list of current MRC publications in the Medical Research Council *Handbook*. In some cases the accessions lists from the library of the organization will be the only source, but publications will be hard to locate. HMSO catalogues are useful for a few non-HMSO publications because HMSO acts as a sales agent for the publications of several official bodies, including those concerned with nuclear energy like the Atomic Energy Research Establishment and the National Radiological Protection Board.

If there is no obvious place where a list of publications of a particular body can be found, it is always worth checking with the library of the organization. Many libraries try to collect all the titles issued by the parent body (though they don't always succeed), and some act as distribution points for such publications. In some cases, however, official bodies issue no lists of their publications whatsoever, and even the library may be unaware of everything that is published.

Listing of new publications

Many of the bibliographical sources discussed so far take a considerable time to record new publications. This detracts from their value because users often need the most recent publications of an organization. It can also create severe acquisition problems as the title may have gone out of print by the time the publications list appears. The bi-monthly issues of CoBOP and the quarterly UKOP disc are the best sources for recent publications of many bodies. The majority of titles are listed quite quickly, though the organization itself may delay submission of information about new titles. In some cases this is to protect their own sales. Regularly revised publications lists, or supplements to less frequent lists, are another possibility. The DoE/DTp *Publications monthly list* supplements the annual publications catalogue by listing new titles, both HMSO and non-HMSO, from the two departments. The appearance of a regular list of new publications in a periodical is also a useful way of locating recent material. Many official bodies have their own periodicals or newsletters and these often include details of new titles: *BRE news of construction research* (six a year) and *CNAA higher education news* (three a year), for instance. Lastly, organizations which make their databases available online or on CD-ROM may include details of recent titles they have published. The *Directory of British official publications* concentrates mainly on separately-issued publications lists and is not so helpful in identifying sources which include details of recent publications. There are many bodies whose recent titles cannot be traced in any of these ways. They will only be found if they appear in general or subject bibliographies and databases.

Databases and other sources

Bibliographic databases and indexing or abstracting services in specialist subject fields may provide an alternative means of tracing the publications of a number of official bodies. Many subject bibliographic sources, particularly those concerned with the primary research literature, try to cover all information sources in their subject area regardless of provenance. It is well worth checking the statement of scope and coverage of bibliographic databases or examining the kinds of materials recorded in printed bibliographies to see whether they include material from official bodies. MEDLINE and *Index medicus* list many of the research publications from the Medical Research Council and its research units since they appear in the primary biomedical literature. ACOMPLINE (and *Urban abstracts* in its printed form) is concerned with local government, but includes many central government publications of interest to local authorities. It is relatively easy to locate details of official material in such online databases because they allow a search by publisher or sponsoring organization. It may be less easy to do so in printed subject bibliographies with their fixed primary arrangement by subject, unless there is a name or organizations index.

A number of databases and printed bibliographies are produced by official bodies and some of these have been mentioned in Chapters 3 and 4. DHSS-DATA on DATASTAR is the record of library holdings for the two departments and has comprehensive coverage of their own publications, including circulars.[8] The facility to search by publication type simplifies the finding of these. IRRD, the International Road Research Database, includes input from the Transport and Road Research Laboratory. Health and Safety Executive publications are included both in the HSELINE online database and the OSH-ROM disc on CD-ROM. The libraries of many official bodies have in-house databases or online catalogues which include their own publications and some of these are also available to external users.

Retrospective coverage

Most of the sources discussed record only the non-HMSO official publications of the last decade or so, though some public bodies have been in existence for over 50 years. Current publications lists are concerned only with new and in-print titles and are usually thrown away when the next issue is produced. Some of the bibliographies of government departments' publications date back to the late 1960s or early 1970s while CoBOP lists material produced since 1980. Retrospective coverage of non-HMSO publications before then depends mainly on inclusion in general and subject bibliographies. BNB and the BNB-MARC database with their patchy coverage go back to 1950. The *London bibliography of the social sciences* (1931 –) was originally a record of the holdings of several London libraries but now covers only the acquisitions of the British Library of Political and Economic Science at the London School of Economics. It is a major bibliography in the social sciences and includes both HMSO and non-HMSO publications under its alphabetical subject headings. The same library has also published the *Guide to government data*, a survey of the non-HMSO and unpublished material held by 12 government department libraries.[9] This is very useful for tracing older non-HMSO publications. A certain amount of non-HMSO material is included in the British Library *General catalogue of printed books*. This is more easily searched in its online or CD-ROM forms. As a last resort the backfiles of annual reports of the individual organization can be searched. The chances of finding most non-HMSO publications before the 1970s are quite poor as there was no general awareness of their significance or even of their existence before then.

References and further reading

1 Hewett, S., 'UKOP – Catalogue of UK official publications', *Refer*, **6** (1), Spring 1990, 28–30; Raggett, P.. 'United Kingdom official publications online and on CD-ROM' in *British official publications online* edited by Valerie J. Nurcombe, Library Association, Information Services Group, SCOOP, 1990, 8–15.

2 Toase, C., 'Official reports: indexes to chairmen of committees', *Refer*, **2** (1), Spring 1982, 10–12.

3 Moss, A., 'The Catalogue of British Official Publications: a reply', *Refer*, **2** (4), Autumn 1983, 9–10; Worthington, D., 'Cataloguing non-HMSO official publications', *GLG newsletter*, **27**, July 1987, 2–4.

4 Richard, S., *Directory of British official publications*, 2nd ed., Mansell, 1984, xiv−xvii.

5 Johansson, E., *Current British government publishing*, Association of Assistant Librarians, South-East Division, 1978, 28; Richard, S., 'The publications of British national para-governmental organizations', *Government publications review*, 5 (4), 1978, 403−4; Tolley, P., 'The Catalogue of British Official Publications under scrutiny', *Refer*, 2 (3), Spring 1983, 4−6.

6 Tolley, *op. cit.*, p.6.

7 Tolley, *op. cit.*, p.5.

8 Smith, D., 'DHSS Data' in *British official publications online* edited by Valerie J. Nurcombe, Library Association, Information Services Group, SCOOP, 1990, 25−9.

9 Comfort, A. F. and Loveless, C., *Guide to government data*, British Library of Political and Economic Science, 1974.

6 The availability of official publications

LIBRARIES AND OFFICIAL PUBLICATIONS

Substantial collections of British official publications have been maintained by many libraries which recognize their importance as records of government policies and decisions and as unique information sources.[1] Until relatively recently these collections have consisted mainly of HMSO publications. There has been scant encouragement from the government for widespread provision and many public libraries had only small collections until the 1950s. No system of depository libraries on the United States model — with complete collections provided free of charge to selected libraries throughout the country — has ever been seriously contemplated by the government. The only concession is the 50% discount for public libraries, which has enabled more of them to provide access to a range of HMSO titles.

Legal deposit libraries

The best collections of British official publications are found in the national libraries receiving them under legal deposit and the Parliamentary libraries. The British Library's Official Publications and Social Sciences Service is the major publicly available collection.[2] It is comprehensive in its coverage of HMSO publications and receives a large proportion of non-HMSO official material; it is weak only in local government publications. Current official publications from the collection are included in the HSS online database on BLAISE-LINE. The OP & SSS recognizes the need to provide positive help to exploit official publications fully. It publishes helpful guides for users like *Parliamentary papers* and the *Checklist of British official serial publications* (q.v.).

The British Library Document Supply Centre (BLDSC) has an Official Publications Section which collects HMSO and government department publications.[3] Most publications from national official bodies are treated as monographs and serials in general stock. BLDSC's role in the SIGLE

European grey literature project has increased the emphasis on collecting reports and local government publications. The BLDSC provides an efficient back-up to local resources for the loan of many British official publications.

Cambridge University Library, the Bodleian Library, Oxford, and the National Libraries of Scotland and Wales all have extensive reference collections of official publications received under legal deposit.

Government libraries

The Parliamentary libraries provide excellent services to Members of Parliament and their research assistants.[4] MPs receive many parliamentary publications automatically and can request copies of most non-parliamentary publications if needed. Emphasis in the House of Commons Library is therefore on access to official information rather than simply providing publications. The Parliamentary On Line Information Service (POLIS) makes such information more easily available. The House of Lords Record Office and the House of Commons Library have the major collections of older official publications from the beginning of parliamentary records.

The libraries of government departments are each major special collections in their own field and are usually available to research workers. Many departments have made special efforts to collect departmental publications and those from associated official bodies. The majority of departments began to issue regular lists of these publications in the 1970s. There has been some reduction in access to government libraries recently. The DTI's Export Market Information Centre (formerly the Statistics and Market Intelligence Library) has reduced its coverage of UK statistics and concentrated its services on exporters, while the Department of Education and Science is considering abandoning its library altogether. The British Library's Science Reference and Information Service issues the regularly updated *Guide to libraries and information units in government departments and other organisations* (29th ed., 1990) which gives brief information on each of these libraries.

Academic libraries

There are several major collections of official publications in academic libraries apart from those in the legal deposit libraries. The great significance of official publications in many of the social sciences and in historical studies and the value of research and technical publications in science and technology have resulted in the establishment of collections of both current and older publications. Most were essentially HMSO collections until relatively recently: over a quarter of university libraries purchase all of HMSO's current publications. Polytechnic and college libraries tend to buy more selectively rather than providing complete collections. The British Library of Political and Economic Science at the London School of Economics aims to be a comprehensive collection of social sciences material, with strong emphasis on both HMSO and non-HMSO official publications. These are catalogued individually and some appear in the *London bibliography of the social sciences*. Warwick University Library is another major collection with a social sciences emphasis. It has a special system of arrangement and is one of the most comprehensively indexed collections. Southampton University Library has the Ford Collection of Parliamentary Papers dating back to 1801. Despite its name this includes non-parliamentary and some non-HMSO publications. It too is well indexed and several useful guides to government publications have been produced.

Public libraries

Public libraries are the only ones currently receiving a discount to encourage them to provide HMSO publications. Just under half of the English authorities but only one in Scotland and none in Wales have complete collections of HMSO publications somewhere within their system. Holdings of parliamentary material in London public libraries can be checked in *Access to parliamentary resources & information in London libraries* (3rd ed., 1988), a useful guide from the House of Commons Library's Public Information Office. Some large city libraries have HMSO publications back to the beginning of this century or even earlier. Coverage of publications from government departments and other official bodies is much poorer. Many public libraries do have publications from local authorities within their area and sometimes from neighbouring areas as part of their local government information services or local collections. There is a need for some official publications at most public library service points, not simply a large central collection. This involves the provision of multiple copies of popular publications, major reports, etc., if the public are to have local access.

Organization and exploitation

All libraries need to consider how best to organize their official publications in the light of users' requirements and the extent and nature of the collection.[5] Many libraries with extensive collections separate

152

official publications from the rest of the stock. This works satisfactorily with some groups of publications, like HMSO material, Ordnance Survey maps and patents, using the arrangement, lists and indexes provided by the publisher. Collections of HMSO publications can follow the *Annual catalogue* sequence with parliamentary publications by category and number and non-parliamentary publications alphabetically by issuing body within the year. The *Annual catalogues* then act as a guide to the collection, eliminating the need for cataloguing, though their inconsistencies in arrangement and deficiencies in indexing affect retrieval. Non-HMSO publications do not form such a coherent group, though CoBOP can provide a guide to identification and arrangement. These collections may be on open access, allowing users to browse, or closed access, which is administratively more convenient, secure and space-saving, but relies on users knowing the titles they require or depending extensively on staff help.

Separate arrangement may be satisfactory for large collections despite the conflict between ease of handling and convenient access, particularly by subject. Libraries with smaller collections may choose to integrate official publications in the normal classified sequence with other material on the same topic. This helps users seeking material on a subject regardless of whether it is official or not, but retrieval of specific documents may be slower. Even some libraries with larger collections have preferred integration for its superior subject approach. The degree of integration will vary from library to library, and there may still be separate files for particular series, pamphlets and leaflets which are not individually catalogued.

The provision of adequate access points to publications is important whatever arrangement is used.[6] Library catalogues tend to have a large volume of entries under 'Great Britain' or 'United Kingdom', creating a maze which few users or even librarians can find their way through. The burden of cataloguing can be reduced by drawing the records from the national bibliographic record, from a cooperative network like BLCMP, or downloading them from UKOP or the HMSO database. Local data (class mark, location) can be added to the record which is then incorporated in the library's own catalogue. Even then, headings may not be consistently applied, while changes of responsibility and of name of official bodies further complicate access. Online public access catalogues allow a greater number of access points through keywords, but vary in the adequacy of their records and software for sophisticated subject searches. Libraries which have chosen not to catalogue official publications may use the searching facilities of UKOP on CD-ROM to trace material since 1980, provided the library's holdings and locations are known. Some libraries have created in-house databases or indexes to provide better access to their official publications collections, for instance by title or subject.

The complexity of official publications, the large number of agencies involved, the peculiar methods of publication and distribution and the frequent changes of responsibility require specialist knowledge of the field if collections are to be exploited fully. Some libraries have specialist posts for official publications librarians, usually where there is a separate collection. This specialist can develop deeper knowledge and help make official publications more accessible to both staff and users. Such posts are vulnerable when budgets are cut or when the specialist leaves, leading to a deterioration in the quality of service, especially if other staff feel that they can ignore official publications.

Specialist staff will be involved in the selection, acquisition, organization and exploitation of the collection. Exploitation includes an enquiry service, formal or informal user education, production of guides and current awareness services, and publicity to draw attention to the collection. Some enquiries will relate specifically to official publications, but all staff need to recognize when more general enquiries, such as transracial adoption, require official material. Many users of official publications are unaware of the range available or how and where to find them. Good sign-posting within the library is essential, as well as published guides. These may be part of a general guide to the library, or separate guides which allow more detail. The latter are important in academic libraries where they may support formal user education programmes. Although basic orientation sessions are normally too brief to do more than mention the existence of official publications, follow-up seminars in more detail may be provided. Much user education in all libraries is informal on an individual basis when a user has a particular information need. Reading lists and current awareness services can help to draw new official publications to the attention of users. Publicity is important if potential users are to know of the collection's existence and scope. This includes publicity within the library as well as external publicity and entries in directories of information resources.

SELECTION AND ACQUISITION
Library selection policies for official publications must take into account the wide range of official publishing organizations when seeking to meet

154

users' requirements and potential needs.

HMSO publications

Selected subscription service

The selection of HMSO publications is relatively straightforward because of the databases, printed lists, and order plans.[7] Large libraries with a wide range of subject interests may use the Selected Subscription Service (SSS), which for a single advance payment (£22,100 in 1991/92) provides single copies of the vast majority of HMSO publications. Statutory instruments may be excluded and either parliamentary or non-parliamentary publications subscribed to as required. About 80 libraries currently subscribe to elements of this scheme. Use of SSS is good value: the total price of publications supplied in 1989/90 was nearly £30,000. It ensures that new publications are received with minimal delay and reduces paperwork considerably. Extra copies can be ordered individually if required after examining the new arrivals. Subscribers need to be aware of exactly what is included and excluded. Main current exclusions are: electronic and microfiche publications; periodicals available on subscription (which includes *Hansard*, *Business monitors*, and the *London gazette*); all agency publications; Northern Ireland publications with the 0 337 ISBN prefix; and *Statutes in force*. HMSO is looking at further categories to omit to avoid a large increase in the subscription. Any library using SSS must ensure that it makes arrangements to receive relevant material outside the scheme.

Standing orders and subscriptions

Libraries (and individuals) with more specialized requirements can use the Standing Order Service. This offers a choice of publications from about 4,000 categories, including agency publications. The choice may be broad, e.g. all education publications; an aspect or type of publication may be chosen, e.g. education statistics, higher education; or the choice may be narrow: an individual series or statutory instruments on a topic. Customers select the groups they require and relevant publications are sent as they appear. This scheme is helpful both to special libraries and to general libraries needing material on specialized topics. There may be uncertainty as to exactly what is included in some categories, however, which could lead to inadvertent ordering of duplicate copies. Periodicals available on subscription are not included in the Standing Order Service. They can be ordered separately and a list with current subscription rates can be found at the back of HMSO monthly and annual catalogues.

Individual orders

Libraries needing relatively few HMSO publications may select each title individually by scanning the *Daily list* or HMSO's Prestel frames. Orders can be sent by post, telephone, telex, fax, or online or on Prestel. Non-parliamentary publications can be ordered in advance of publication from *At press* (q.v.), but parliamentary publications are never available before their release date and time. Libraries close to HMSO bookshops may select from shop stock, though this will not be the full range of publications. Alternatively libraries may order through an HMSO agent, local bookseller, library supplier, or subscription agent for serials. HMSO has become much more efficient at supplying orders quickly since its Publications Centre opened in 1983, with average supply time falling from 17 days in 1981 to five days in 1990.

Non-HMSO publications

Despite some problems with HMSO, its system is well organized, smooth and efficient when compared with the difficulties experienced in selecting and acquiring many non- HMSO publications. UKOP and the *Catalogue of British official publications* provide a straightforward way of identifying a significant proportion of the output. They are a great help, whether the library simply wants to know that the publication exists and the address from which it can be obtained, or whether it takes advantage of the document delivery service. This provides microfiche copies of many publications listed in CoBOP for a flat rate charge. Fiche can be ordered individually (which is expensive), in subject groups like food or education, or in collections of Science and Technology or Social Sciences material. Although this means paying for quite a number of free publications, it greatly simplifies acquisition, saves staff time and reduces supply costs.

Many non-HMSO publications, however, are either not included in the document delivery service or not listed in CoBOP and UKOP at all. These have first to be identified, using the sources described in Chapter 5, and then ordered individually. Some official bodies like the Ordnance Survey and the BBC have agents and commercial outlets and their publications are available from the library's usual book-trade suppliers. Most offer no trade discount and their publications will be handled reluctantly, if at all, by booksellers and library suppliers. Libraries may have to make their own arrangements to acquire much of this material.

For many organizations the only way to obtain a publication is to write to the exact section, or even precise room number for government departments, enclosing cash with the order where appropriate. Even this does not guarantee that the publication will be received as it may be out of print before it is listed. Sending cash with order can be a problem for libraries as an invoice is normally required; publicity stating the price of the publication is often accepted as a substitute, however. Some bodies, like the Welsh Office, will invoice on request, but others will not. Some will accept lump sum deposits in advance for future publications, which simplifies payment. It is unwise to rely too much on being placed on a mailing list as it may be revised and your request discarded before the next edition or issue is due. Standing orders may not be accepted by the body, necessitating repeat orders every time a new edition is published. If publication is regular and predictable this is merely inconvenient; but if titles appear irregularly the requesting library is put in a very difficult position.

Trying to obtain many non-HMSO official publications can be time-consuming, frustrating and costly. The fundamental problem is that many official bodies do not see themselves as publishers and therefore do not provide the facilities to simplify ordering and supply. Nevertheless, ordering is considerably easier now than it was in the past because some non-HMSO publishers have become more professional about the way they publish and distribute their titles, often centralizing ordering and distribution. The Scottish Office Library Publications Sales Service, for instance, was established in 1981 to act as an enquiry point for all Scottish Office publications and to coordinate their sale.[8] It accepts standing orders and subscriptions, lump sum deposits in advance, and has computerized its ordering and stock control. On the other hand, there are still too many examples like the DTI publications despatch centre for export publications which does not hold all export-related material from DTI, will not accept subscriptions or standing orders, and restricts the majority of titles to DTI Service Card holders!

SCOOP

The Standing Committee on Official Publications (SCOOP) is a subcommittee of the Library Association's Information Services Group which provides a forum for discussion between official publishers and librarians. Its membership includes representatives from many Library Association Groups and other bodies like Aslib, the Committee of Departmental Librarians and SCONUL. It works to improve access to and availability of UK official publications and takes up both matters of policy and of detail. Special emphasis is given to the bibliographic control and distribution of official publications. SCOOP's concerns include local government publications as well as HMSO and non-HMSO material at the national level. In 1990 it set up a working group to tackle the issues and problems relating to European Communities' (EC) publications. HMSO regularly consults SCOOP on changes and developments and SCOOP makes representations direct to those responsible for other official publications. The main committee meets twice a year and has working parties on non-HMSO official publications and local authority publications, as well as on EC material. SCOOP organizes seminars to make librarians aware of developments in official publishing, like *British official publications online* in 1989, and the proceedings of these are published. It also publishes directories and guidelines, including the *Directory of specialists in official publications* (2nd ed., 1988). Regular news of SCOOP's activities can be found in *Refer*, the ISG journal (three issues a year), which also reviews new SCOOP publications and has articles and notes on current developments in official publishing. Since its inception in 1971 as the HMSO Services Working Party, SCOOP has provided an invaluable channel of communication which has led to many improvements in access to British official publications.

Copyright

The availability and use of information in official publications is affected by copyright legislation. The Copyright, Designs and Patents Act 1988 introduced a new category of 'Parliamentary copyright', administered by HMSO for the titles they publish. Greater freedom is allowed in reproducing some parliamentary material because of its unique nature. *Hansard* may be freely photocopied. Substantial extracts (up to 30%) of statutory publications, but only brief extracts (up to 5%) of other parliamentary papers, may be copied without seeking permission or paying a fee. Longer extracts or the complete text of statutory material and parliamentary papers may be copied three months (statutory instruments) or six months (bills, acts and parliamentary papers) after the date of publication. Non-parliamentary publications and non-HMSO material from government departments and many official bodies are covered by Crown copyright. This includes the individual maps and charts of the Ordnance Survey and the Ministry of Defence (Hydrographer's Department). Normally permission is required to photocopy even brief extracts of these publications and a fee is charged, except for free departmental information material. Users registered with the Copyright Licensing Agency are covered by the terms of their licence. A letter giving advice on photocopying conditions is available from HMSO. These conditions apply to photocopying by libraries and individuals; commercial reproduction is subject to separate licensing arrangements.

When the publishing body wants the information in a publication to be widely available, it will waive Crown copyright and include a statement that the publication may be freely reproduced. Users may be allowed to make multiple copies when the issuing organization is only able to supply a single copy of the document.

References and further reading

1 Smith, B., 'British official publications III. Accessibility and use', *Government publications review*, **6** (1), 1979, 11−18; Cherns, J., *Availability and use of official publications in libraries*, Unesco, 1983. (This deals mainly with the acquisition and organization of official publications.)

2 Howes, R., 'Official publications in the British Library', *International library review*, **19** (3), July 1987, 225−41; Hamilton, G., 'The Official Publications Library and the British Library's services for law', *Law librarian*, **16** (1), April 1985, 16−19.

3 Wood, D. N. and Ekers, A., 'Official publications at the British Library Lending Division', *Interlending and document supply*, **11** (1), 1983, 17−20.

4 Englefield, D., *Parliament and information*, Library Association, 1981. (For details of the House of Commons and House of Lords libraries and the House of Lords Record Office.)

5 Goodwillie, J., 'The development of bibliographic control of official publications in Trinity College Library, Dublin', 87−97; Gorman, G. and Downey, J., 'Bibliographic control of official publications at the Institute of Development Studies, England', 125−45; Pemberton, J., 'Official publications in a new bibliothecal context', 147−72 in Pemberton, J. (ed.), *The bibliographic control of official publications*, Pergamon Press, 1982. (Despite its title, this book is concerned mainly with the organization and handling of collections of official publications in a number of libraries worldwide.)

6 Gibbons, K., 'Cataloguing of government publications', *GLG newsletter*, 27, July 1987, [4−5].

7 *Getting HMSO books*, HMSO, 1990.

8   Hills, P., 'Scottish Office' in *Who publishes official information on statistics?* edited by Valerie J. Nurcombe, Library Association, Information Services Group, SCOOP, 1989, 66–70.

7 *Local government publishing*

Local authorities in Britain are producing an estimated 50,000 documents a year on topics ranging from planning and social welfare to civil defence and local history. This is the greyest of the grey area of official publishing with only limited bibliographic control at present. In the past local government publishing has often been written off as small scale and of little importance except in the immediate locality, or as largely a matter of internal documents produced for committees and councils. The reorganizations of local authorities, measures like the Local Government (Access to Information) Act 1985, and the principle of public participation in planning decisions have resulted in more attention being given to some aspects of local government publishing. Increased recognition of the sheer quantity of documents produced also makes them harder to ignore. To appreciate the nature and significance of local government publishing requires some knowledge of the system of local government in Britain, the kinds of work for which local authorities are responsible, and the ways in which their documents can be used. This is followed by an examination of the range of publications produced, their availability and bibliographic listing.

THE LOCAL GOVERNMENT SYSTEM

Structure
The institutions of local government in this country are ancient: many counties can trace their origins to the shires of the Saxon kingdoms while self-governing towns date back to at least the medieval period. The idea of an organized system of local government providing services and administering each area of the country, however, first became a reality in the late 19th century. The Local Government Act 1888 created county councils and gave the larger towns county borough status independent of the counties. The second tier of local government administration, the

urban and rural district councils, was established by the Local Government Act of 1894. This structure endured until the reorganizations of local government in London in 1965, Northern Ireland in 1973, England and Wales in 1974, and Scotland in 1975.

The present structure of local government in Britain has considerably reduced the number of local authorities, creating larger units which are more capable of providing adequate services. The 47 county councils in England and Wales provide strategic and countywide services. They have a second tier of district councils with more local responsibilities. The 36 metropolitan districts and the London bodies — 32 London boroughs and the City of London — are single-tier authorities responsible for all services since the abolition of the Greater London Council and the metropolitan county councils in 1986. Scotland has a mainly two-tier system with nine regional councils and 53 district councils, though Orkney, Shetland and the Western Isles have single all-purpose authorities. Northern Ireland has 26 district councils with limited powers. Major services are administered by area boards for education and libraries and health and personal social services which are responsible to central government departments. In total there are currently over 500 councils in the UK, each with a range of departments. Further reorganization creating single-tier authorities throughout the country is likely to be implemented by the mid-1990s.

Every local authority is controlled by a democratically elected council, the councillors each representing a particular ward or electoral division and serving normally for four years. Councils have a number of specialist committees and subcommittees for different groups of services which are advised by the chief officers for each service. Local authorities employ over two million people who administer policy and provide services, including administrators, professional people, technical and clerical staff and manual workers. Their activities are financed partly by loans for capital expenditure and by a mixture of government grants, local authority income and revenue from the community charge to meet current expenditure on salaries, supplies, services and debt interest.

The relationship between central and local government is changing, with central government exercising much greater control over how local authorities spend their money. Services are being partially or wholly removed from local authority control: education is the major local service, but in 1989 the polytechnics and many higher education colleges became self-governing institutions, while further education colleges and schools may opt out of local authority control. Over a million council houses

162

have been sold to their tenants since 1980 and the 1988 Housing Act gives remaining council tenants the right to have their homes controlled by a landlord other than the local authority. Other services like refuse collection have been privatized in many areas. Limits on local authority trading activities are being introduced which will reduce their sources of income.

Fuller information on the structure and financing of local government can be found in the latest edition of *Britain: an official handbook* or in Tony Byrne's *Local government in Britain* (5th ed., Penguin, 1990).

Functions and services

The powers and duties of local authorities are derived from Parliament and are laid down in many Acts of Parliament and delegated legislation. The legislation may place a statutory duty on the local authority to provide a service, as in the case of school education, or it may be permissive, allowing the authority to provide the service only if it wishes. In addition the local authority acts as the enforcement agency for national legislation, including consumer protection laws. In two-tier authorities the range of local government functions is divided between the county or regional and district councils on the general principle that services which are best planned for a large area are dealt with at county level (such as strategic planning and roads) while more local functions (e.g. environmental services, housing and local planning matters) are dealt with by district councils. In discussing individual services the division of responsibilities between first- and second-tier authorities is indicated. The metropolitan districts and London boroughs are each responsible for almost the whole range of services for their area, except for public transport and police.

Education is still the major local government function in terms of expenditure. Local authorities provide primary and secondary schools, colleges of further education (but not universities and polytechnics) and any special provision required for children with mental or physical handicaps. They also offer many adult and continuing education courses. Teachers and support staff are employed by local authorities, which are also responsible for grants for students in higher education. Their role in education is diminishing as schools and colleges choose to opt out and control their own budgets and policies. Local education authorities provide youth clubs and centres and employ youth organizers who work alongside voluntary organizations and coordinate youth work in the area.

Planning is another major local government responsibility. Most development requires planning permission and must be in accordance

163

with the structure and local plans for the area devised by the planning authority. Strategic planning is a first-tier function in counties and regions and each council must have central government approval for its structure plan. District councils are responsible for preparing local plans for their area (within the context of the structure plan) and dealing with local planning applications for developments ranging from infill housing to new shopping centres. Local planning authorities are also involved in matters affecting the physical environment like tree preservation and footpaths. Positive measures to help develop the local economy, to stimulate employment and improve living conditions are being taken by many local authorities through economic development initiatives. Unlike planning this is not a statutory requirement, but Economic Development Units or Departments are now widespread.

Roads, traffic planning and transport are mainly local government responsibilities. The Department of Transport looks after motorways and trunk roads, but most other roads are administered by county or regional councils which deal with their construction and maintenance. Traffic planning and regulation, parking and road safety measures are also a county function. District councils maintain some minor roads and provide car parks. Local bus services which were formerly run directly by local authorities are now operated by public transport companies in many cases. Some areas have passenger transport authorities responsible for setting policy for public transport. Public transport in London is the responsibility of London Regional Transport, now classed as a nationalized industry.

Personal social services became an expanding local government responsibility following the Local Authority Social Services Act 1970 which imposed new duties on local authorities. The National Health Service and Community Care Act 1990 expanded local authority responsibility for the community care programme. Services are aimed at elderly people, those with physical or mental handicaps, children at risk, families with social problems, and the homeless. Help includes the provision of residential homes and day care facilities, home care for elderly and disabled people, and advice on personal and social problems. Local authorities employ qualified staff in their homes and centres and social workers to deal with individual cases. In England and Wales the probation service is separately administered locally by special committees of magistrates and co-opted members, whereas in Scotland local authority social workers also undertake this function.

The fire service and the police are special functions administered by separate authorities with local councillors serving on each committee.

Both services may cover more than one local authority area, in which case a joint committee is set up. The West Midlands Police Authority and the West Midlands Fire and Civil Defence Authority both cover the whole of the West Midlands county with its seven district councils. The fire service is concerned not only with firefighting but also enforces fire prevention legislation and has civil defence responsibilities. The Metropolitan Police Force in London is responsible directly to the Home Office.

Housing and environmental services are both the responsibility of district councils. They own and maintain the remaining stock of council houses and flats and build new ones. They have wide powers for housing generally to deal with unfit housing, enforcement of the building regulations, payment of house renovation grants and assessment of rents. Many local authorities provide a housing advisory service to deal with people's problems with housing matters of all kinds. Environmental health officers embody local authority responsibility for public health matters like food quality and hygiene, control of pollution, refuse collection and pest control. The district councils act as an enforcing agency for public health legislation. County councils have a similar role in consumer protection legislation with trading standards officers enforcing trade descriptions and weights and measures legislation. Some councils run consumer advice services to deal with shoppers' queries and problems.

The final group of local government services are often brought together in leisure services directorates. The public library service is a first-tier function in counties. The provision of art galleries and museums and support for local arts groups including theatres and orchestras are the responsibility of both first- and second-tier authorities, depending on local arrangements. Local authorities provide land and facilities for sports and recreation: parks, playing fields, swimming baths and sports centres. They are concerned with the promotion of tourism in their area and with the provision of tourist information.

PUBLICATIONS

Value

This extensive range of functions and services inevitably generates a large volume of publications. Many are initially for internal communication between officers and committee or between staff at headquarters and those in other parts of the area. Policy documents and reviews are prepared for council and committee meetings, and councillors may require further information to support policy decisions. Since the passing of the Local

Government (Access to Information) Act 1985 the public has a right to attend all council, committee and subcommittee meetings. They can also inspect the agendas, minutes, reports and background papers relating to business discussed in public. In addition, the commitment to informing the general public and involving them in decisions requires many publications to explain council policy and future plans, to publicize existing achievements and to invite discussion and opinions. Publications are one of the means used by local authorities to demonstrate to the community that they are efficient, economical and effective. They can also be used to generate income. Many documents like planning studies or social work reports must be disseminated to district council planning departments or local casework teams. Good communication between different departments of the council and between county or regional and district councils in an area is essential, especially as schemes may involve joint action.

Local authorities tend to consider the use of their documents only within the authority itself or by the public in the area. Many publications have a much wider value which is not fully realized. Local authorities frequently face similar kinds of problems in planning, social work, education and other spheres. The plans and proposals of one authority may be very useful to another, avoiding considerable potential duplication of effort. Statistics, data and reports from one authority can be helpful to similar authorities for comparative purposes. Sometimes even the initiative shown in publishing a particular title will suggest the need for other authorities to produce similar publications. Local government officers are frequently very keen to find out what other authorities are doing while being reluctant to publicize their own activities.

Local authority publications are useful in higher education both for students of local government administration and in professional courses for social workers, teachers, engineers or planners who will need to be aware of current developments. Such publications will be raw material for student projects and case studies and for research for higher degrees. The research value of local government publications should not be overlooked, especially in view of the extensive research activity in many local government departments. It is far too easy to write off these publications as being of local value only when their wider exploitation is hampered by problems of identification and access.

The range of local government documents and publications can be divided into a number of main groups which will be produced by most local authorities. In the examples cited, the abbreviations CC for County

Council, DC for District Council, BC for Borough Council, M for Metropolitan and LB for London Borough are used.

Table 7   Local government documents and publications

Council and committee documents	Planning documents
Administrative reports and statistics	Economic development publications
Byelaws	Publicity and promotional material
Technical and research studies	Advisory publications
	Tourist information
Policies and guidelines	Local history publications
	Bibliographic sources

Council and committee documents

Every local council, committee and subcommittee produces minutes of its meetings and agendas for its next meeting. The minutes form a comprehensive record of the local authority's decisions and actions. Any council has a considerable number of committees and subcommittees, making it difficult to keep track of minutes from all of them. The minutes may not be very meaningful to the general public without background information which is normally provided by the local press. Councillors have access to policy papers, reports and background papers prepared by officers to help them make decisions. These have been publicly accessible since the Local Government (Access to Information) Act 1985 came into force but some councils deter enquiries through high copying charges. It is also, perhaps, no coincidence that in many local authorities the important political decisions are now taken in private meetings of the ruling group rather than in public in full council. The minutes and agendas are normally available for consultation in council offices and public libraries where they are regularly scanned by some members of the local community. They may also be available for sale on subscription.

Relatively few authorities index their minutes to make searching easier. Indexing is especially important in those authorities, mainly London boroughs, which issue few separate publications but create a single complex serial from their agendas, minutes and reports to committees. As this material records current council policies which must be put into effect by departments, the creation of policy files or databases seems essential for effective internal management let alone for public information.

167

Administrative reports and statistics

Annual reports are useful information sources for the public, summing up the activities of the authority over the past year, with sections on each department. The need to demonstrate local accountability has affected the way this information is presented. Many authorities produce attractive and informative annual reports with colour illustrations and easily understood statistics. They include the annual accounts of income and expenditure for the previous year and a series of performance indicators for services. Individual departments produce their own reports initially for submission to the council, but copies may also be circulated to the local press and interested members of the public. These are more detailed than the council annual reports and often have supporting statistics and illustrations, but they are not usually so well produced. Annual reports extend beyond those produced by departments: the governing bodies of state schools must produce reports which are widely distributed among parents.

Comparative statistics for local government are compiled and published by the Chartered Institute of Public Finance and Accountancy (CIPFA). Individual local authorities publish their own statistics in various ways. Some produce general statistical yearbooks covering everything from debt charges to swimming bath admissions, as in the annual *Birmingham statistics* (Birmingham City Council). Statistics are also found in council yearbooks and diaries, as are the names of councillors and dates of council and committee meetings for the next year. More specialized statistics may be produced like the *Annual population forecasts for Oxfordshire* (Oxfordshire CC) or the monthly *Unemployment statistics* from Sheffield City Council.

All councils must produce annual financial statements and details of the budget for the forthcoming year. Basic financial information is circulated to the public with the community charge bills and summary publications like Southwark's *Budget book* are produced annually.

Byelaws

Byelaws are made by local authorities under powers granted by Parliament. They have the force of law but apply only to the area for which they are made and must be published to be operative. They are used to prohibit nuisances such as cycling on footpaths or fouling by dogs, or to regulate conduct when using facilities provided by the local authority such as parks and art galleries. They must be confirmed by a government minister and copies are made available by the local council.

168

Technical and research studies

Local authorities generate a considerable amount of technical and research literature, usually to provide evidence or feasibility studies as a basis for policy decisions. Like central government departments, they may set up working parties to gather information and report back on particular problems. Technical studies are initiated to assess issues affecting the council like the *South Warwickshire housing study. Market assessment and effects of the M40 extension* (1988) jointly undertaken by Warwickshire County Council and two district councils. One study which no one would wish to see implemented is *Transition to war. NATO mobilization and emergency powers: the implications for civil defence and local government* (1989) from South Yorkshire Fire and Civil Defence Authority. Although many studies are carried out by council staff, consultants are employed in some cases: the study of *Video libraries: the potential for public/private sector partnership* (1989) was prepared by Capital Planning Information on behalf of Devon County Council.

Many authorities carry out surveys to measure quantifiable facts or to assess opinions: surveys of the use of recreational facilities or of the needs of people with physical handicaps, for instance. Surveys are particularly likely to be carried out by planning, housing and social services departments, e.g. *10% household survey 1987* (Redditch BC, 1987), *Local housing condition survey 1988* (Nithsdale DC, 1988) or the *Report on survey of people with mental handicaps in the City and Hackney Health District* (LB of Hackney, 1988). Departments may initiate research into problems which involve the collection and analysis of data from sources like the census, publications of other local authorities or reports of research institutes, universities and colleges. This research may be carried out in centralized research and intelligence sections or in departmental units.

The decision as to whether and how to publish these technical and research studies rests with each local authority. Since many exist to support the council's policy initiatives the reports may be produced mainly for the committee or chief officer with few additional copies available for other enquirers. The research may never be written up as a full report: it may be incorporated into the papers of a working party or a chief officer's report to committee. Even when the report is separately published it may receive little publicity. Some potentially valuable research remains unknown despite the existence of research listings and databases and information exchanges.

Policies and guidelines

Any local authority must determine its policies on a wide range of matters from planning issues like the siting of takeaway food shops to the provision of nursery schools. Planning policies and the publications relating to them form a distinct group of local government publications and are discussed separately. All other departments have policies, sometimes collected in policy files, which are updated following new committee and council decisions. Policy statements may be useful to other authorities: Nottinghamshire County Council's policies on *Libraries in primary schools* (1984) and *Library resource centres in secondary schools* (1985) are of national relevance.

Staff must be given guidelines on how to act in specific circumstances. Two examples from Social Services Departments are *Departmental policies and guidelines for staff on the sexual and personal relationships of people with a mental handicap* (Hertfordshire CC, 1989) and *Dealing with violence. Guidance to staff on violence by clients* (Dorset CC, 1988). Equal opportunities and race relations policies have received much attention in recent years and many councils have issued policy statements and guidelines on these topics.

Planning documents

The largest group of local government publications amounting to over 10% of the total output are those associated with the planning process.[1] Britain has a comprehensive system of land-use planning and development control and local authorities have a statutory obligation to produce development plans. These are of two types: structure plans setting out the general policies for development and land use which are prepared by county and regional councils; and local plans giving detailed guidance for development within a particular area which are produced by district councils. Single-tier authorities like the metropolitan districts are now adopting unitary development plans combining general policies with detailed proposals on aspects like housing, shopping and the environment. Government proposals in 1990 to abolish structure plans have been abandoned, but in future they will concentrate more on strategic issues and contain less detail. Planning departments normally have research units to carry out the investigation and monitoring necessary to form the basis of development plans and for their revision.

Structure plans

One structure plan involves the preparation of many documents. Initially research is carried out and background papers on aspects like transport and conservation are produced. The proposals are prepared and publicized and the public invited to express their views. A *Public participation statement* must be submitted to the Environment Minister with the plan to show that consultation has taken place. Subject plans support the main structure plan by dealing with policies on special aspects like coastal development, mineral extraction or conservation. Structure plans have been completed for most areas and the *Approved plan* published. These must be kept under review to update them in the light of changing circumstances and this generates further publications like *Tourism priority areas. Cumbria and Lake District joint structure plan alteration* (Cumbria CC, 1988).

Local plans

Local plans are produced within the broad framework of the policies laid down in the structure plan and relate to a specific area like the *Skewbridge local plan* (Lincoln City Council, 1989). Nearly 1,500 local plans are in preparation or have been adopted. Every district council is involved in producing several local plans for different areas within its district. The contents of these plans are specified by central government and require several documents during the approval process. First, there is a consultation document setting out the main issues and choices. The draft proposals are then published: *Oxford fringe and greenbelt local plan. Draft for consultation* (Vale of the White Horse DC, 1988). Public reactions to the plan are summarized: *Beccles area local plan. Report of publicity and consultations* (Waveney DC, 1989). The plan is deposited with the Department of the Environment in the form of a written statement and proposals map. If there are any objections there may be a public enquiry, the report of which will be published. When the plan is adopted (possibly with modifications) the approved version is published: *Hoddesdon town centre approved local plan, 1988* (Broxbourne BC, 1988). Even this is not the end of the process as, like structure plans, they must be monitored and reviewed: *Islay, Jura and Colonsay local plan. 1st review and alteration and monitoring report* (Argyll and Bute DC, 1988). Local plans may also include subject plans on aspects like shopping policy and recreation. There is even a *Peat local plan* (1989) from Somerset County Council. Areas scheduled for extensive redevelopment in the structure plan are the subject of action area plans, though there are relatively few of these.

171

Other publications

County and regional councils are obliged to publish their transport policies: *Leicestershire transport policies and programme* (Leicestershire CC, 1988). They must submit an annual statement to central government on transport policies and costs, with a programme for the next five years. One of the critical issues facing development plans is the availability of land for housing. This involves studies of the need for house-building and the production of plans: *East Lothian housing plan, April 1989—March 1994* (East Lothian DC, 1989, 2 vols). Planning departments are also often involved in economic development strategies and projects (q.v.).

Apart from publications which are a statutory requirement, planning departments produce a range of other material. Guidance for developers is provided in planning handbooks e.g. *Lechlade planning policy* (Cotswold DC, 1988); design guides like the two from Delyn Borough Council in 1988 on *House alterations and extensions* and *Shopfronts and their advertisements*; and recommendations like Glasgow District Council's *Good practice guide: environmental improvements to local authority tenemental housing* (1988). Public information booklets and leaflets deal with how to make a planning application, planning appeals and requirements affecting developments like access for the disabled or parking. Details of major development proposals may be circulated to increase public awareness and invite comments: the *Solihull High Street development* (1989) proposals are explained in an illustrated brochure. Environmental policies have become politically important and councils are adopting environmental action plans. The issues involved have to be communicated to local people through publications like *The environment in Avon* (1990) which incorporates a questionnaire on environmental priorities. Planning departments collect statistics to monitor development plans and carry out research studies and surveys. They often have their own publications unit to deal with production and distribution of the material produced.

Economic development publications

Local authorities are concerned to develop the local economy and to support local businesses. This may involve the creation of an economic development unit or may be undertaken by the planning department in association with other departments. The local authority may take joint action with other bodies in central and local government partnerships and cooperation with the private sector. European Community funds, notably the European Regional Development Fund (ERDF), are used to stimulate economic development: Birmingham alone received nearly £60 million from the ERDF between 1984 and 1988.

An economic development strategy for the area may be formulated and published both in full and in summary form. Studies of particular aspects of the local economy are carried out, like *The local economy and 1992* (Wakefield DC, 1989), which is one of a series of *Occasional papers in economic development*, or *The manufacturing sector in Edinburgh: employment trends in the 1990s* (City of Edinburgh DC, 1988). Statistical publications monitor the state of the local economy: the *Labour market information bulletin* from Birmingham's Economic Development Unit analyses local employment and vacancy trends.

There is fierce competition among local authorities to attract new businesses to their area. Several have substantial budgets and specialist staff with regular advertising, promotional videos, booklets and periodicals all produced in a highly professional way to heighten awareness of the Peterborough effect or to persuade people that they would rather be in East Kilbride. More traditionally, industrial handbooks for the county or district provide information about existing industry, transport and communications and other local facilities, like the *Gwynedd industrial directory*. Some authorities publish directories of local firms, e.g. Bedfordshire's annual *Business guide* and the *Bromley business guide* (1990). Conferences and exhibitions held locally can also boost the local economy. A number of authorities have sophisticated conference and exhibition centres like the National Exhibition Centre and the International Convention Centre which are owned by Birmingham City Council. Those with more modest facilities will also seek to promote them through publications like the *Northamptonshire meeting, conference & exhibition guide* (Northamptonshire Tourism, looseleaf).

Assistance to local businesses and encouragement of those considering starting businesses is the third element in economic development. Courses, seminars and advice are offered and these must be publicized through newsletters like *Birmingham business today* (Birmingham City Council, quarterly), which also gives current information on events, opportunities and support for local businesses. Information on the help available may be brought together in publications like *An A-Z guide to assistance for business in Devon & Cornwall* (Devon County Council, 1989). Help may also be given to the unemployed through such publications as the *Job seeker's guide* (LB of Hammersmith and Fulham, 1988), while Southwark Council's *More choice, better workforce* (1990) provides guidance to employers on recruitment.

Publicity and promotional material

Every local authority puts out a considerable amount of publicity about its activities and services. This includes not only leaflets, newspapers and books but videos and databases as well. There are frequently revised general guides to the council's services like Birmingham City Council's *Your Council services*. These list each department and section outlining its responsibilities and showing who to contact. Departments may publish a general guide to their services, like *A guide to the social services department* from Dudley or the *Environmental health and trading standards handbook* (1990) from Solihull. They also produce leaflets on individual services and common problems: what to do with old cars, housing care and repair schemes, help from the education advice service, or a guide to the public library and its services. There are many leaflets and booklets on matters like rent allowances, councillors' advice sessions, services for disabled people in the area or facilities for pre-school children. In areas with large ethnic minority groups leaflets may be provided in several different languages.

The leaflets and booklets are relatively ephemeral and must be revised frequently. They tend to be distributed through the public departments of the local authority and by voluntary organizations: libraries, civic information centres, neighbourhood offices, and Citizens Advice Bureaux. A number of councils provide this kind of ephemeral information in electronic form through local viewdata systems.

Some departments or sections of the local authority issue regular newsletters to publicize activities or events. Museums, art galleries and libraries often issue details of talks, exhibitions and meetings in this way, e.g. *News and events* (Birmingham Museums and Art Gallery, bi-monthly). The work of the local authority or of a particular department may be presented on video which can be shown to local groups. Quite a number of local authorities publish a civic newspaper which is distributed free to the public to show what the council is doing and what its future plans are. Examples include *Harlow news* (Harlow DC, monthly), *Stockport civic review* (three a year) and *Your Solihull* (Solihull MBC, three a year).

Advisory publications

Just as central government issues advisory material, so too does local government, although not in such profusion. Publications aimed at helping local businesses have already been mentioned. Many trading standards/consumer protection departments offer advice on consumer matters like the series of booklets from Avon on *Avoiding the pitfalls of* . . . , e.g. home improvements or car purchase. Housing advice is also common, e.g. *Condensation remedial measures* (LB of Southwark, 1988), and doesn't just come from housing departments: *Private tenants – your rights* (1990) is an information pack published jointly by Gateshead Libraries and Gateshead Law Centre. Several departments issue guides to help people with disabilities, including advice on *Getting around* (1990) by public transport from CENTRO, the West Midlands Passenger Transport Executive. There is even a guide to cooking your Christmas turkey from Solihull's Environmental Health Department. Some advisory material is aimed at the authority's own staff: *Shared reading* (1988) is a guide for teachers while how to deal with *Aggressive girls* (1989) is for social services staff; both titles are from Hertfordshire County Council.

Tourist information
Local authorities advertise their area through a range of tourist literature. Local guidebooks extolling the delights of the area and advertising accommodation, shops and services are the mainstay of this literature. The major resorts publish annual guides, but other councils may produce theirs less frequently. Many district councils have their official guide produced by one of the commercial publishers specializing in this field, such as the British Publishing Company. Guidebooks can be a good source of recent information about the area with facts and figures, a brief history, local government services, hospitals and churches, sports facilities, industry and usually a street plan or map of the area. More specific information is usually available in a range of leaflets and pamphlets which may be free or available at a nominal charge. These deal with what to do and see in the area, local walks, nature trails and town trails, guides to houses and sites open to the public, where to stay or eat, etc. *Guided walks in Sussex* (1990), for instance, is a substantial booklet jointly published by East and West Sussex County Councils. Many local authorities produce regular listings of events giving details of current plays, films, musical events, meetings, exhibitions and talks. Public libraries often publish guides to local societies and organizations with addresses and details of activities. Like most tourist publications, these must be regularly updated and may be available in electronic database form. Guidebooks for the main holiday resorts are well

publicized and available in many libraries throughout the country, but much tourist literature can be obtained only within the local area.

Local history publications

Publications about different aspects of the area in the past, its people, institutions and events are often produced by local authorities. They have become useful sources of income as they find a ready market if they are well publicized and some titles sell thousands of copies. They range in form from pamphlets and books to prints, photographs and calendars. Some authorities sponsor a series of historical studies of their area, such as the Bristol series or the Portsmouth papers from their respective city councils which include topics like *Portsmouth breweries, 1492 – 1847* (1988) or *The story of HMS Bristol* (1986). Many local authorities publish histories of the council and its activities. The centenary of the establishment of county councils in 1988 produced a number of studies like *Centenary: a hundred years of county government in Norfolk* (Norfolk CC, 1989). Individual local government departments and sections may also publish histories of their work.

The most prolific publishers of local history sources are usually the education department, public library service, local museums, art galleries and record offices. Several education departments publish material to support the teaching of environmental and historical studies in schools by relating them to the local context. *The Jacobites in Manchester, 1745* (1986) from Manchester City Education Department is a typical example. Libraries have a long tradition of publishing local history material based on their special collections. These include prints, photographs and postcards, e.g. *Westbury in old photographs* (1988), a collaboration between Wiltshire Library and Museum Service and the local history publisher Alan Sutton. Specially written booklets, exhibition catalogues and extensive books are also produced. Examples include *Croydon Airport – the Australian connection* (LB of Sutton, 1988), *The Redding pit disaster* (Falkirk DC, 1988) and *Felix Gluck 1923 – 1981* (LB of Richmond upon Thames, 1988). An indication of the amount of material produced is given by *Scottish local studies resources* (Scottish Library Association), the 1988 edition of which lists 340 books and pamphlets from 35 public library services. Libraries are often responsible for bibliographies of books, pamphlets and periodical articles about the area, for instance the annual *Sussex bibliography* (East Sussex County Library).

Local museums and art galleries publish a range of materials similar to those at national level (q.v.). Many of their publications relate to artists, collections, sites or buildings in the area, e.g. *Four artists explore coalmining* (Swansea City Council, 1986) or *By hammer and hand. The Arts and Crafts Movement in Birmingham* (Birmingham Museums and Art Gallery, 1984). Record offices too may publish guides to their collections of local archives, calendars and lists of special collections, and other material like *The memorandum book of Richard Cholmeley of Brandsby, 1602–1623* (North Yorkshire County Record Office, 1988) or the more popular *Kill or cure* (Staffordshire Record Office, 1987), which is a collection of 16th- and 17th-century medical remedies.

Bibliographic sources

A substantial number of bibliographic sources are produced within local authorities, mostly by the library service. The need for current awareness services, short reading lists and more extensive bibliographies to improve awareness and use of information by councillors and local government workers has been recognized. Many public libraries and information units within other departments produce periodicals contents bulletins, indexing services and abstracting bulletins. A few are issued daily (e.g. *Today's press* from Cheshire County Library), while others are weekly or monthly lists of recent articles, reports and books of general local government interest (e.g. *Birmingham briefing*) or aimed at a particular department like the fortnightly *Social work information bulletin* compiled cooperatively by three Midlands authorities.

Reading lists, bibliographies and other publications for different groups of users are produced by public libraries. The *Westminster union list of periodicals* (new ed., 1990) reveals the extensive backfiles held by Westminster City Libraries. *Beyond words* (Birmingham Library Services, 1990) is a guide to a selection of black writers, while *East London in fact and fiction* (Redbridge Libraries, 1990) is an annotated bibliography of books about the area. Catalogues of special collections in libraries are occasionally issued like the *Catalogue of works by and about T.E.Lawrence in Dorchester Reference Library* (Dorset County Library, 1990). A number of public libraries support and publish writing by local people: *50 botanical travellers* (1990) is a collection of poems from the National Garden Festival published by Gateshead Libraries.

Electronic information

Although most local government documents are still in printed form, there is a growing use of electronic databases. Several authorities have their own viewdata systems like Gloucestershire's THEMIS and

KINGTEL from Kingston upon Thames with details of councillors, events, local tourist information, etc. This information may be publicly accessible through terminals and touch screens. In many authorities in-house databases have been created on microcomputers and on the local authority mainframe computer for information ranging from statistical data to directories of community organizations. A few bibliographic databases have been developed like Cheshire Local Government Information Service's database of books, articles and local government publications. An increasing number of public libraries have online public access catalogues of their stock.

Much of this electronic information is not readily accessible outside the authority, although some councils are using standard electronic mail systems. In many cases printed publications are derived from the databases, although these may not be updated as frequently as the database itself. Local government information in electronic form is an even greyer area in terms of access and identification than printed local government publications!

BIBLIOGRAPHIC CONTROL AND AVAILABILITY

Publishing practice

Relatively few local authorities have a general policy on publishing and a central organization for making their publications available. Devon is one of the exceptions and was the focus of British Library supported research studies of its publications programme and their marketing.[2] A number of other authorities, or individual departments, have also recognized the potential for income generation from a well-organized, carefully chosen and properly marketed output. Some have successfully marketed their publications directly, while others have cooperated with commercial publishers to take advantage of their publishing expertise and established distribution network. Official guides have long been produced for councils by specialist publishers, but recently other material, notably planning information handbooks, have also been issued in this way. Educational, historical and other material is now co-published like the *Somerset thinking skills course* (1988) from Blackwell in association with Somerset County Council, or *Science horizons* (1988) from Macmillan Education and West Sussex County Council.

In the majority of authorities publishing is almost totally decentralized and uncoordinated, except in some individual departments like planning. As a result not even the originating authority has a clear picture of its own publishing output. Publications lists are quite common among national public bodies but are still rare in local government. Even when they do exist they may omit such vital information as price, date and how to obtain the publications. People seeking a document must know the precise department and section responsible for it, assuming that they are aware of its existence in the first place. With a few exceptions, mailing lists are unreliable and the only way to ensure a continued supply of publications is by regular reminders to the department concerned. Although this is feasible on a limited scale, it is a hopelessly time-consuming and uneconomic way of tracing publications.

Little thought may be given to the production of publications. The number of copies printed is often insufficient to meet demand, and any wider interest may not be welcomed partly because it increases costs. Publications may lack the most elementary bibliographical details, particularly date of publication and price. Many local authorities do not consider what they produce to be publications or are ignorant of the legal requirement to deposit copies with the British Library's Legal Deposit Office. Kennington's study showed that only a small fraction of the estimated output is deposited.[3] This severely hampers bibliographic control and the wider availability of publications.

In an attempt to remedy this situation SCOOP's Local Authorities Official Publications Working Party has produced *Guidelines on the preparation of local authority official publications* (LA, ISG, SCOOP, 1989). This argues the case for a clear and well coordinated publications policy and shows that much of what is produced by local authorities, including minutes of meetings open to the public and papers discussed at them, would be considered as publications. It gives advice on the bibliographic and other information which should be included in a publication and on production, costing, marketing and distribution. The Working Party aims to improve bibliographic control of local government publications and access to them by encouraging legal deposit and the development of a national database.

At present it is difficult to consult the full range of publications from most authorities. Few have a central point where all publications can be obtained and there may be strong resistance to such centralization. Some departments and sections regularly send their publications to the public library, especially when titles are felt to be of wide public interest. This is voluntary and covers only a small proportion of the authority's output. Access through the library is essential as the local community has a right to be able to find out what their local authority is doing. County

179

libraries have the added difficulty of trying to obtain publications from all of the district councils within their area as well as those of the county council. Public libraries are much less well placed than government department libraries to be aware of what is being published by their parent organizations. Most do offer a local government information service, however, and the librarians responsible for these services are in many cases actively seeking out publications.[4]

In a few instances material for distribution to the public may be sent to all households. Basic information about the authority and its activities is included with community charge bills. In some places council services are decentralized with area or neighbourhood offices providing a range of services and information, including publications. There may be an information centre which helps people to get in contact with the right department or section: this too carries a range of publications from the authority, particularly directories and guides to services and other information leaflets. Council and committee minutes are available for consultation, usually in the Chief Executive's department and in public libraries. Many publications can only be obtained from the specific department responsible for them and the existence of much of this material remains unknown to most people, including others working for the same local authority.

Major bibliographies

Knowledge of the existence of local government publications and access to them can be significantly improved if there is adequate bibliographic control. Currently this is limited and probably less than ten per cent of the output is listed by the major bibliographies collectively. Planning documents are the best covered area, but even here the listings are nowhere near complete. For other types of publications those recorded in bibliographies represent only a small fraction of the total output. This is partly because many items are still not regarded as 'publications' by the originating authority despite their potential value.

A number of major bibliographic sources, printed and online databases, include local government publications within their scope. The *British national bibliography* (and BNB-MARC database) lists about half of the local government publications received by the Legal Deposit Office, the others being rejected as outside its scope. It records 300−450 titles a year and is strongest in its coverage of planning documents and historical material.

The British Library Document Supply Centre has collected grey literature for many years. Since 1980 it has placed special emphasis on collecting local government publications, using Capital Planning Information as a collecting agent. Coverage of technical and research studies is stronger than in BNB. This material is listed in the monthly *British reports, translations and theses* (BRTT) in broad subject categories.[5] Much appears in the subdivisions of Group 05: Humanities, Psychology and Social Sciences. Retrieval by the name of the issuing authority is more difficult and the subject keyterm index can be idiosyncratic. Material recorded in BRTT is also input into the SIGLE database. This is a European cooperative database which aims to improve access to all types of grey literature. SIGLE records are quite short but offer more flexible searching than BRTT. Material from local authorities can be traced under the name of the body. SIGLE began listing this material in quantity in 1980 and reached a peak of just under 1,000 titles a year in 1984 and 1985. It is very slow to include new material, probably because of the difficulty of getting it quickly from local authorities.

ACOMPLINE, the bibliographic database of the London Research Centre's Research Library (the former Greater London Council Research Library), covers books, pamphlets, reports and especially articles from all sources on a wide range of local government topics.[6] As a result it has a substantial number of users among local authorities and is publicly available through the host ESA-IRS. Local government publications form a small proportion of its entries. Its records are fuller than those on SIGLE and include a brief summary of subject content for each document which is particularly useful in improving subject searching. *Urban abstracts* (monthly) is the main printed service derived from the database. A series of alerting bulletins are also based on ACOMPLINE and the local government news database URBALINE on topics like finance (fortnightly), the environment (weekly) and Europe (monthly). URBALINE is useful for its coverage of press releases mentioning policies or publications from most London boroughs. ACOMPLINE has a bias towards the South-east in the local authority material listed, although input from the Local Government Training Board has broadened its coverage. The LRC Research Library is willing to develop it as a national database of local government publications if individual authorities submit records for inclusion.

Urbandoc news records a significant number of local government publications. It is a monthly current awareness service from Capital Planning Information which covers all aspects of local government. It lists about 400 local government publications a year with good coverage of planning and economic development publications as well as a significant amount from education, social services and housing departments.[7]

Specialized listings

The major bibliographies cover a broad range of local government publications, but there are also specialized databases, indexing and abstracting services listing material on particular aspects of local government. The DHSS-DATA database on DATASTAR and the monthly *Social service abstracts* (HMSO) contain details of some publications from local authority social services departments, although their main emphasis is on books and articles on social policy and administration. The Local Authorities Race Relations Information Exchange (LARRIE) is one of a number of specialist databases and information centres on matters of local government concern. It was set up in 1984 to collect material from local authorities on race relations. It offers a free telephone enquiry and document supply service to local authorities and from 1989 is also publishing a quarterly current awareness bulletin, *The LARRIE digest*. PLANEX is the database of the library of the Planning Exchange in Glasgow and is available for direct online access or on ESA-IRS.[8] It has a comprehensive coverage of Scottish planning, housing and economic development documents and also includes relevant material from the UK as a whole. The Planning Exchange also publishes current awareness services and offers enquiry and consultancy services. It is able to provide material which more general collecting agencies would have difficulty in finding out about.

Periodicals in some professional fields with strong local government links may record relevant local authority publications felt to be of interest to their readers. Planning journals are useful for their coverage of at least some of the many planning documents from local authorities. The *Library Association record* mentions material from public libraries in its news or reviews sections. General local government periodicals like the *Municipal journal* and those from the local authority associations are also sometimes useful in this way.

The growing amount of research carried out by local authorities has led to the development of research databases and registers. *Current research in Britain* (British Library, annual) widened its scope several years ago to include local government projects. The Institute of Local Government Studies (INLOGOV) publishes an annual *Register of local government research*. Direct online access to this is planned via

ACOMPLINE. The Local Authorities Research and Intelligence Association (LARIA) is the body for those involved in local authority research and publishes the quarterly *Research & intelligence news* with articles and news items about current research. More specialized research listings include the Society of County Librarians' *Register of research and investigation* (Essex Libraries, 5th ed., 1989) and the quarterly *Social services research* from the University of Birmingham Department of Social Policy and Social Work.

Details of bibliographies, current awareness services, databases, research registers and other publications relating to local government matters can be found in *Local authority information sources. A guide to publications, databases and services* (2nd ed., SCOOP, 1989). This lists over 40 such services with information on scope, content and availability.

Future developments

The fundamental problem with local government publications is that their value is still not fully recognized even by the authorities producing them. Consequently there is no great incentive to improve bibliographic control or to make them more easily available. The British Library Document Supply Centre has been collecting and listing a substantial number of local government publications since 1980, but use of them remains low. SCOOP has been actively concerned with local government publications for several years. It has organized seminars, issued publications and produced guidelines. It is currently seeking to persuade chief executives of the importance of their publications and at the same time is offering practical guidance to improve them. In 1989 SCOOP launched an initiative to improve bibliographic control by basing a national listing of local authority publications on the ACOMPLINE database. If local authorities follow SCOOP's recommendation to use their public library or local government information service as a depository for all publications then those libraries can prepare entries for inclusion on ACOMPLINE. This seems a realistic way to improve coverage beyond the current low level. However, progress in the first year of the initiative was slow and anything approaching complete coverage is a very long way off. A complementary strategy is to encourage the further development of the specialized information exchanges, each collecting or listing local government publications in their own subject area and offering information about them to staff in all authorities. At present most of them are relatively recently established and their collections, databases and listings cover only a short period of time. They may meet the needs of local authority specialists better than the more general listings covering all aspects of local government.

References and further reading

1   Nuttall, B., 'The views of users: academic users', 14−18; Rickman, E., 'Departments of the Environment and Transport', 48−52 in *Access to local authority official publications* . . . edited by Valerie J. Nurcombe, Library Association, Reference, Special and Information Section, 1985.
2   Kennington, D., *Local government publications: their packaging and marketing*, Devon County Council for British Library Research and Development Department, 1982 (BLRD report 5745); Capital Planning Information, *Devon County Council publishing programme*, British Library, 1984 (BLRD report 5803).
3   Kennington, D., *Access to local government documentation*, British Library, 1981 (BLRD report 5619). A summary of the findings of the report is also available: Kennington, D., 'Access to local government documentation', *Interlending review*, **9** (4), Oct 1981, 118−21.
4   A list of these local government librarians is included in *Local authority information sources. A guide to publications, databases and services*, 2nd ed. compiled by Mary Robinson, SCOOP, 1989, 50−73.
5   Chillag, J., 'British Library, BRTT and SIGLE' in *Access to local authority official publications* . . . edited by Valerie J. Nurcombe, Library Association, Reference, Special and Information Section, 1985, 40−4.
6   Barton, J., 'ACOMPLINE and URBALINE' in *British official publications online* edited by Valerie J. Nurcombe, Library Association, Information Services Group, SCOOP, 1990, 45−56.
7   Duvall, J., 'Local government information services', *Aslib proceedings*, **40** (2), Feb. 1988, 33−42.
8   Watson, I., 'The collection and availability of local authority official publications' in *Access to local authority official publications* . . . edited by Valerie J. Nurcombe, Library Association, Reference, Special and Information Section, 1985, 6−13.

Index

This index includes organizations, types of publications and some individual titles (such as bibliographic sources) which are discussed in sufficient detail to make reference to them worthwhile. No attempt has been made to index the hundreds of titles and organizations briefly referred to as examples. Government departments are indexed under their subject word (e.g. 'Energy, Department of') where references to their work and publications are brought together. The reading lists at the end of each chapter are indexed with the page number followed by 'r' and the item number e.g. 43r7. Letter by letter alphabetization is used for the filing order.

190